Sokule...
This is NOT Your
Grandmother's
Social Media Site...

Written and compiled
Jane Mark - President of Sokule Inc
Phil Basten - Developer of Sokule

Sokule: This is NOT Your Grandmother's Social Media Site

ISBN 10: 1-933817-64-X
ISBN 13: 978-1-933817-64-4

Published by: Profits Publishing
http://profitspublishing.com

Canadian Address
1265 Charter Hill Drive
Coquitlam, BC, V3E 1P1
Phone: (604) 941-3041
Fax: (604) 944-7993

US Address
1300 Boblett Street
Unit A-218
Blaine, WA 98230
Phone: (866) 492-6623
Fax: (250) 493-6603

Foreword...

By Frank Sousa

Social Media platforms like Facebook, YouTube, Twitter and dozens of other popular Social Media sites are changing the way business is being done on the net. Sokule is the next generation of Social Media.

Businesses need to connect with targeted audiences in order to increase sales and they need to do it quickly, effectively and repeatedly.

Sokule was developed with this in mind and has taken Social Media to the next level. Its users can post to over forty Social Media sites instantly and brand their name at many of the mostly highly visited sites on the net.

Social Media has become a highly effective way to increase sales, cut advertising costs, and to communicate directly with consumers. In *Sokule... This is Not Your Grandmother's*

Social Media Site, authors, Jane Mark and Phil Basten together with some of the founding members of Sokule; guide you through the use of their site in easy to follow steps.

They lay out, in words and screen shots, just how you use this masterfully designed advertising tool to grow your own online business. You can start at the beginning and read it through or just pick out the chapters you are interested in pursuing. By the time you have finished, you will have a complete understanding of Social Media and how to make it work for you.

Frank Sousa
Co-Developer and founder of Traffic Geyser
http://sokule.com/trafficgeyser

Table of Contents

Prologue...

Who are you?

Tell me in 140 characters or less...

If I had to tell you who I am in 140 characters or less, I may tell you that...

"I'm a Social Media nut who loves to post messages but hates having to log into a number of different Social Media sites to make those posts."

Or, I might say...

"Jane Mark, NYC. I run an advertising agency online and I can change the way your story ends."

Or perhaps I could say...

"If I could show you how to make a lot of money online without doing a lot of work, would that interest you?"

I bet I got your attention with that one. :-)

I may possibly say something like...

"I am a dreamer, an innovator, a bit of a nut who likes to have fun but is dead serious about business."

Or, I may well say,

"I built a Social Media site, made it profitable from day one, and now I am sharing it with you."

I could say any or all of these things, in drips and drabs, and I could do it in 140 characters or less. I can tell you a bit about myself and who I am.

Let's put it this way.

Many people know me. I have made millions of dollars online and I can show you exactly what I do. If you do what I do, you can make money too. It's simple. If you want to read my bio you can do that here... It's the usual stuff but it's good if you need to know more: http://www.sokule. com/about.html

However, if you want to pick my brains, then read this book: Sokule... This is NOT Your Grandmother's Social Media Site.

Whoops; that post might be a bit more than 140 characters.

But no worries; I didn't make this post on Twitter. It's too long.

I didn't make this post on Facebook either; I would have had to log in to do that, and that takes up too much of my time.

I didn't do it on MySpace. I can never figure out where to go when I get into MySpace and some guy from my area is always popping up saying he would like to meet me.

I kid you not. Every time I log in someone tries to pick me up.

I don't want to be picked up. :-)

So I made this post on Sokule, because I can do it without any hassles.

Bottom-line.

My partner, Phil Basten, and I are in the Online Advertising Business. We have been making a substantial living online for the past ten years.

About two to three years ago we noticed online advertising was changing focus. Twitter and Facebook and MySpace and dozens of other Social Media sites had sprung up, and businesses by the thousands were testing them out.

We knew that if we wanted to keep up with the times and grow our business, we would have to do the same, but that meant having to log into all of the major Social Media sites, make our presence known, and recruit our clients one by one.

Or would we?

Maybe there was a better way, an easier way, to keep our name and our business in front of the millions of people we wanted to reach.

So, Phil and I decided that...

- If we wanted to say something that was a bit longer than 140 characters...

- If we wanted to make a difference on the net and help our business friends get the recognition they need...

- If we didn't want to spend the rest of our lives logging in and out of here and there and making the same post over and over again at various sites...

- If we were not interested in being picked up by every Tom, Dick, and Mary...

- If we wanted everyone in the universe to know who we are, but we didn't want to spend all day in the 'Getting to know you' mode...

... Then we better develop a site where we could do exactly what we wanted to and do it automatically.

That's how Sokule (pronounced So-Cool) was born.

I warn you...

Sokule is not your Grandmother's Social Media site. It is light years ahead of many of the biggest and most popular sites on the net.

So sit back and relax while we show you how we use Sokule to build relationships and make sales...

It's an eye-opening experience and you'll love it.

Jane Mark
President, Sokule, Inc

Track us on Sokule
http://sokule.com/postit/sokule

Acknowledgements...

This book is a collaborative work.

We could not have done it without the help of our wonderful members who work with Sokule every day and contributed to this book. They took time out of their busy lives to share their Sokule experience with you. You will get to know them through the chapters they have written.

Chapter 6 – Hey Buddy, Can You Spare a Soken...? - Gabriella DArko
Chapter 10 – Pre-schedule – Make posting easy... - Kathy Pleasance
Chatper 12 – Climbing the Walls – Sokwall and Kule Wall... Nina Spelman
Chapter 17 – Direct Message (squeek) all trackers... - David Merrington
Chapter 22 – How to Stand Out From the Crowd... - David Merrington
Chapter 25 – Sokule, So What? – A theme is born... - Jenny Rogan
Chapter 29 – Sokule Success Stories... – Jeananne Whitmer

... our appreciation also goes to Tom Haley, Peter Watson, Jimmie Rose Bryant, Jenny Rogan, and Richard Brewster who contributed their Sokule success stories.

We also wish to give huge thanks to Ron Davies, as well as David and Sue Preston for helping us in the beginning.

Their knowledge of Twitter gave us many unique insights and helped Sokule become what it is today.

A special note of thanks also goes to good friends like Frank Sousa, Willie Crawford, and Mike G. for helping us to get Sokule out of the gate quickly when we launched, as well as, huge thanks to all our wonderful Sokule members who make our days joyful on the net and have helped make Sokule the success story it has become.

Jane Mark
Phil Basten
Sokule, Inc

Introduction...

When I think of Social Media sites like Twitter, Facebook, and MySpace, I think work. I think, OMG, it's time to log in; answer messages; post this message to one and that message to the other; chat with Fred, Bill, or Cynthia; listen to the latest videos posted; respond with a cheeky reply and...

Yikes! Who has time to do all that?

I belong to over three hundred Social Media sites and the list grows daily. If I had to log in to each one every day and post something, I would run myself ragged, run out of things to say, and end up grumpy at the end of the day.

Would I have accomplished anything?

Who knows? I would have to log back into each Social Media site and check to see if anyone responded to me. At the end of the day, all I may have done is a lot of logging in and chatting, without having really achieved what I wanted to.

So I thought to myself...

Wouldn't it be great if I could just log into one place and post to all my favorite sites with one click. A place that looked and acted a little like Twitter, so it felt familiar and so I didn't have to get used to a whole new scene.

A place where I could make one post and it would instantly appear on Twitter, Facebook, MySpace, and thirty-six other top Social Media sites and blogs.

A place where I could edit my messages, so they look professional, and I could save face if I misspelled a word(I am notorious for misspellings). :-)

A place where I could post messages that were longer than 140 characters. I do have some important things to say at times.

A place where I could post to sites where I didn't need any friends or followers to start with but my posts could still be seen by new people all over the world.

I knew I could do a lot of these things at Twitter and Facebook, but that also meant I would have to go outside my favorite Social Media sites to third-party sites and pay extra for things like...

• Being able to: Auto-welcome my followers.
• Direct squeek (email) all my followers.
• Find out who is talking about me and my sites.
• Add videos to my site.
• Add clickable links to sites I promote.

So building my own site seemed like the logical choice. I could do what I needed to and make money doing it.

I could post an article and have a shortened version of it appear on all my favorite Social Media sites with a link back to my main post.

I could add an affiliate program and pay my members to advertise the site for me.

And, I could make my Social Media site profitable from day one, not just for me, but also the members of my site.

Wouldn't that be cool...?

Wouldn't that be a dream site?

Well, my partner Phil and I built that site. It took nine months, but it was well worth the wait. Sokule is now a highly popular, business-oriented, Social Media Site where you can...

- Log in.
- Make a post.
- Click one time, and...
- Presto. Your message is all over the net in a nanosecond.
- You can post to Twitter, FaceBook, MySpace, and thirty-six other Social Media sites instantly with one click.
- You can add images and videos and graphics to your posts.
- Your posts can be as long as you like.
- You can edit your posts.
- You can re-squeek and re-tweet your favorite posts at the same time.
- You can pre-schedule your posts. Up to twenty-five at a time.
- You can direct message all your followers one at a time, or upgrade and reach them all with one click.

- You can earn commissions, even as a free member, when you introduce someone to Sokule and they upgrade under you.
- And lots more.

http://sokule.com/

Sokule is changing the way people do business on the net.

In the chapters that follow, we are going to show you exactly how to use Sokule to change the way your story ends.

We have a lot to cover, so grab a cup of coffee, put on your reading glasses, and let us show you why Sokule is not your Grandmother's Social Media site. Which is another way of saying it's not what you think.

Chapter 1 – So What is Sokule?

Post – Ping – Profit...

Sokule is a business-friendly Social Media site with the primary task to help businesses and individuals get the exposure they need to get noticed quickly on the net. It looks and acts a little like Twitter, which means that when you start using Sokule, you feel at home. But that is where the resemblance ends.

Sokule is business friendly...

It is designed so that any small business or individual can quickly and easily set up their business presence, and spread the word instantly with one click.

So how does Sokule work?

1. Sokule is a posting site.

Sokule posts automatically to Twitter, FaceBook, MySpace, and thirty-six other Social Media sites and blogs. All you need to do is login to your account, post your message, and it instantly appears on Twitter. Twenty-five to thirty minutes later, it will appear on more than forty Social Media sites and blogs, including your own blog.

Sokule is a highly effective Social Media advertising vehicle, but it does way more than just carry your post to other Social Media sites.

2. Sokule is a pinging site.

When you make your post, Sokule will ping the weblogs for you.

Now what on earth does that mean?
Here, take a look at this site...
http://weblogs.com

Are you there yet?

Watch what happens for a few minutes. Every second you will see a new post appear. Those posts or messages are being spidered by the search engines every second, as their robots scour the internet looking for fresh content. If you make an interesting post that solves a problem, chances are pretty good that the search engines will pick it up and rank it highly.

Weblogs.com is just one ping site. Members who use Sokwall can ping thirty-two additional top weblog sites at the same time. Even if you never post on any other Social Media site, your post on Sokule will ping the weblogs and the search engine robots will find your new content.

Now don't fret if you don't understand this part yet. I know it seems a bit technical, but believe me, you want your posts spidered by the search engines. It is just one of many ways you can get highly targeted traffic to your site.

No other Social Media site, at least that we are aware of, does this for you. Sokule helps you create the buzz on the net that gets your business noticed fast.

Now we are going to show you how to use Sokule effectively and how to make your posts zing.

You can join Sokule free or you can you join as a paid member.

Paid members earn larger commissions, but even if you join free, you can still earn commissions. We pay everyone who makes sales for us. Very few Social Media sites allow you to earn money by referring others.

Let's say you introduce Tom to Sokule. He signs up under your affiliate link and upgrades to a Silver membership. You get paid on Tom's upgrade.

Sokule pays out thousands of dollars each Friday. That's right, you make the sales and we'll cut you a check weekly. You can put some of that Green Spending stuff in your pocket, starting today.

So sign up now and...

Post – Ping – Profit.

That is what Sokule is all about...
http://sokule.com

Now let's go over all of the moving parts and applications that Sokule offers you.

You can read the following chapters in order or skip to whichever chapter talks about the applications that interest you.

This is not a "read once, put it on the shelf" dust collector.

You'll want to keep a copy right next to your computer so you can open it and go straight to the section you need when you get stuck somewhere.

So, are you ready to take a new look at Social Media?

Sokule is not your Grandmother's Social Media site. It was built for business by business people to meet your online business needs.

Chapter 2 – Where Do I Start?

Sokule is a business-friendly Social Media platform. You can use it to connect to other like-minded people and get your business noticed quickly and effortlessly.

Even though there are many parts to Sokule, it is still easy to get off to a fast start. Just follow the steps below and you'll be an expert Sokuler before you can blink.

Step 1 - Your profile...

Your first step is to add your profile. People want to know something about you. So login to your account and click on the 'settings' link at the top of the page. Fill in your profile and click 'save,' then go to the commissions section and give us a way to pay you. Next, add your picture, add your bio, and make your first post. Now you are ready to rock and roll.

Step 2 - Invite people...

In Social Media, the rule is that the more people you have following you, the better your results will be. Sokule has a number of built-in systems you can use to get trackers or followers. The first of these is to use the 'invite' tool and invite people from your existing email accounts. These are people with whom you have had prior contact or a prior relationship. You'll find the 'invite' tool in your members' area in both the 'settings' section and on the right hand side of the main members' control page.

Step 3 - Post a welcome message...

First impressions count, so make your first post a good one. Go to the post message box and post a short welcome message. This is the first thing people see when they come to your 'postit' page, so make your message warm and inviting. Do not throw an advertisement at people at this stage.

Step 4 - Go to the icon that says Sokens and click it...

Now click "claim Sokens" and start tracking other members of Sokule. This is another great way to gain followers fast. It works on the law of reciprocity. I follow you and you return the favor at some point and follow me.

Step 5 - Offer Sokens...

Go to the "offer Sokens" page and make a compelling offer so people want to track or follow you. This is another fast way you can build your list of followers or trackers.

Step 6 – Set up your Twitter account...

Free members: set up your Twitter account and enter your Twitter username and password in the Twitter box section so your posts from Sokule instantly appear on Twitter.

Paid members: go to the Social Media box at the bottom of the members' control page and set up your posting sites so that your posts from Sokule appear on all the Social Media sites you belong to. You can add up three different Twitter accounts.

Step 7 - Tell others about Sokule...

The best way to tell others about Sokule is to tell them where you advertise and what tools you use at Sokule. Most marketers are on the lookout for good places to advertise, so don't be shy—send them your affiliate link. You will find your affiliate links at the top of your members' area.

Step 8 - Visit the training section of Sokule...

The training section gives you an overview of the site and how it works, and the videos walk you through each of the applications. Many of your questions will be answered in the FAQ section of Sokule, so be sure to visit that section too.

These eight simple steps will give you fast start to your journey at Sokule.

In the next few chapters, we will go into some depth about some of the most important applications you can and should use at Sokule.

You can read the chapters in any order you like.

If you are new to Sokule, you may want to go through the chapters one by one so you get a handle on the full power of Sokule. If you are an old hand at Sokule, you may want to just skip to the sections that interest you.

So poke around and have some fun and you'll soon see why Sokule is not your grandmothers' Social Media site...

Chapter 3 - Membership Levels...

Sokule is free to join. If you are new to Social Media sites, this is probably a good place to get your feet wet. Look around, test different aspects of Sokule, and when you begin to understand the enormous power of Sokule, then consider upgrading.

If you managed to get a copy of this training handbook and you are not a member of Sokule, you can join free here... http://sokule.com

Sokule has six membership levels.
- Free
- Bronze
- Bronze Plus
- Silver
- Gold
- Founder

Each membership level gives you more Social Media sites to post to, higher commissions, more state-of-the-art marketing tools, more ways to communicate with your trackers (followers), and even more ways to make money.

As you look through the various membership levels, you may come across applications you are not familiar with. Just scroll down to one of the chapters that talks about that application to get a clearer picture of what it does.

For now, let's go through some of the important differences in the various membership levels.

Free Membership...

Free members get a site that looks very much like a Twitter site. It is the basic membership, but you can do most things you can do at Twitter and a bit more.

- You can put up a short bio about yourself.
- You can include a live link to your site.
- You can make 140-character posts that instantly appear on Twitter.
- You can use the Sokens (credits) tool to get followers.
- You can use the birthday card tool to build relationships.
- You get 5,000 Sokens (credits) when you sign up.
- You get 25 Sokens (credits) when someone signs up under you at Sokule.
- You get two affiliate pages you can advertise and earn from.
- You earn 20 percent commission when someone you introduce to Sokule upgrades under you.
- A free member's page at Sokule looks like this...

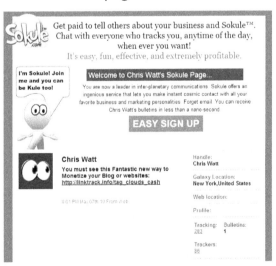

Bronze Membership...

This is our basic $9.95 monthly membership.

This is a good way to start increasing your reach at Sokule. You can always add on applications to your monthly membership as you decide which ones are must haves for you.

- Bronze members get everything that Free members get including the following nifty additions.
- You can edit your posts at Sokule, so if you make a spelling mistake, you can correct it right away. I mispell everything (including the word misspell) so this tool is a godsend for me. :-)
- You can add up to five live links to sites you own or promote.
- You can add up to five Social Media sites you want others to join, like FaceBook, Twitter, MySpace, and so on.
- You can post 500-character long messages, which is a really kule feature.
- You can rotate up to five different profiles. Present different aspects of your business and see which one gets you the most trackers (followers).
- Post on Sokule and you also post on your Twitter account and four other leading Social Media sites.
- You get 10,000 Sokens on sign up.
- You get 100 Sokens every time someone signs up under your link.
- You earn 30 percent commission when someone you introduce to Sokule upgrades under you.

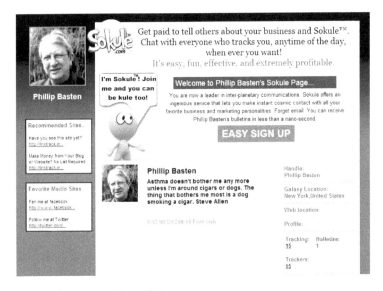

Bronze Plus Membership...

This is our 'grab the lot' $49.95 monthly membership.

Here is where the rubber starts to meet the road. With a Bronze Plus Membership, you get many of Sokule's most powerful applications. You get everything Free and Bronze members get with these very kule additions.

- Your posting power just increased substantially. You can now post to Twitter and fourteen other leading Social Media sites.
- You can add videos and graphics to your postit page and create a professional business presence.
- You can auto welcome all of your trackers (followers).
- You get to direct squeek and email all of your trackers every three days with one click.
- You can use Sokwall, which lets you make article-length posts and have these posts appear on Twitter,

Facebook, MySpace, and the other twelve sites you can post to.

- You can add images to your squeeks (posts).
- You can use Keyword Alert to spy on your competitors.
- You can use the ReSqueek and ReTweet buttons on your own website.
- You can pre-schedule up to twenty-five posts in advance.
- You can add ClickBank products to your postit page. It's a passive way to generate some extra income.
- You get 25,000 Sokens (credits) on sign up.
- You get 150 Sokens every time someone signs up under your link.
- You earn 30 percent commission when someone you introduce to Sokule upgrades under you.

The Bronze Plus Membership really gets you into the ballgame at Sokule.

Silver Membership...

This is our $197.00 annual membership. If you snap up the OTO when you signup, you can save $100.00. If you upgrade later through the member's area, it will cost you $297.00.

Whether you pay $197.00 or $297.00, this is one of the best value buys you can get at Sokule. You get everything that Bronze Plus Members get but you save a whole lot of dough by paying once a year instead of monthly and you get these goodies...

- You get to post to a total of thirty Social Media sites including Twitter, Facebook, and MySpace.
- You get 125,000 Sokens (credits) when you sign up.
- You get 250 Sokens every time someone signs up under your link.
- You earn 40 percent commission when someone you introduce to Sokule upgrades under you.

Gold Membership...

This is a three-year membership for just $697.00.

You get everything Silver Members get with these additions...

- You get 250,000 Sokens (credits) when you sign up.
- You get 500 Sokens (credits) per sign up.
- You earn 45 percent commission when someone you introduce to Sokule upgrades under you.

Founder Membership...

This is a one-time payment. The current price is $1799.00. This is our premium membership level. You pay once and that's it.

Only 1,500 Founding Memberships will ever be sold at Sokule...

At the time of writing this book, the first 500 were sold at the launch price of $1299.00. The second 500 are now selling at $1799.00 and, when these are sold, the price will go up to $2499.00.

When those are gone, it will be too late. The curtain will come down and the party will be over.

Here is what you get as a Founding Member...

- You get 50 percent commission on all personal sales. This is our highest commission level.
- You get access to every Sokule application we add for life and we have at least two years' worth of applications on the drawing board right now. As a Founder Member you get them all as part of your membership.
- A special Founder Members' seal on your postit page. This sets your postit page apart from other members and helps you sell Founding Memberships, which can help put a nice chunk of change in your pocket. You can see that seal on my page here. - http://sokule.com/postit/sokule

- You get early notice of any Sokule-related site that we develop that has an affiliate program so you can tell your lists before the rest of the world hears about it. This can help you get the jump on others and put serious cash in your pocket.
- You get two permanent business listings in the members' area of Sokule. You can post your own business here, as well as edit or change your offers whenever you like.
- You can post your messages to every Social Media site we add to Sokule. The current total is more than forty sites. This is where the real power of Sokule lies.
- You get 1 million Sokens (credits) when you upgrade, which you can use to get trackers (followers) fast by making a high Sokens offer.
- You get 1,000 Sokens (credits) per sign up.

This is, without doubt, one of the best advertising deals we have offered on the net in ten years. Make sure you take advantage of it.

Sokule offers everyone a chance to earn commissions online. No matter which membership level you choose, you can introduce others to the site and when they upgrade, you get paid.

Sokule is Not Your Grandmother's Social Media Site. We pay our members to tell others about our incredible site.

Chapter 4 – Show Me the Money...

If you have been watching the Social Media site explosion closely, you should have noticed a number of sites like MySpace, Facebook, and Twitter have really grown their memberships to enormous sizes by telling their members to go out and invite others to become part of these communities.

There was no charge to join these sites. All were free. They all grew to enormous size in a relatively short period of time.

The business model for these Social Media sites is to grow a huge database and then use the demographic information provided by the members to sell advertising to businesses large and small.

A huge database can be a very valuable asset for any company and this business model is one way to go if you are starting a Social Media site online.

At Sokule we chose a different business model.

Our philosophy is that if you bring someone to our site and they pay money for a service at Sokule, then you should get a piece of the action.

We built in an affiliate program so we could pay members who told others about us. If someone signs up under your affiliate link, and then they upgrade at some point at Sokule, we will cut you a check for that upgrade.

It's as simple as that.

Anyone at Sokule can earn a commission, even our free members, plus...

The commission rate varies from 20 percent to 50 percent depending on your membership level, but our position is clear. You bring us a paid member and we are going to show you the money.

Another thing we decided was to pay our members once a week on Friday. A lot of sites make you wait thirty or sixty days, but that can be devastating to small marketers and home business owners. At Sokule we eliminated that. Most people like weekly checks, and we enjoy writing them.

That means you could literally make Sokule your full-time business on the net by simply telling others where you advertise. Tell them about the tools you use at Sokule and don't be afraid to show them the benefits of upgrading.

You can earn some large paychecks if you sell a Silver, Gold, or Founder membership each month, plus you can earn monthly residual income when you sell Bronze, or Bronze Plus memberships.

Let's take a look at the kind of commissions you can earn with Sokule.

Example 1: You are a free member earning 20 percent per sale.

Let's suppose you sign up a Bronze member at $9.95 per month. You will receive $1.99 per month as a commission each and every month that this Bronze member remains active.

Now let's suppose you get an annual Silver member upgrade ($297.00) under them. You would receive 20 percent of that annual silver upgrade, or $59.40, and you will receive that each and every year as long as the Silver member remains active.

Now let's suppose you get a Founder upgrade at $1799.00. You would earn a one-time commission payment of $359.80. That's one heck of a chunk of money just for joining up at a site for free, right?

Example 2: You are a Founder member earning 50 percent per sale.

If you sign up a Bronze member, you would earn $4.98 per month from that sale. If you sold 100 monthly memberships at $9.95 over the next twelve months, you would have a nice monthly income of close to $500 per month.

If you sell a Silver membership, you would earn $148.50 per year from that sale. If you sold 50 yearly memberships at $148.50 per year in the next twelve months, you would have a nice annual income of around $7,425.00.

If you sell a Founder membership, you would earn a whopping $899.50 one time from that sale. If you sold just 10 Founder memberships at $1799.00 each over the next twelve months, you would pocket $8,995.00.

These numbers may seem high, but they are not that difficult to achieve at Sokule. Many people sign up free at first to look around and get used to the site. As soon as they see that it makes sense to use the applications that we are discussing in our book, they upgrade.

So you are going to get upgrades if you tell people about Sokule and what you do each day at Sokule. That means you can get paid every Friday. All you need to do to get paid is enter your payment information in the commission area of the members' area. You'll find this in 'settings.'

Make sure you enter an online payment processor like PayPal or AlertPay in your profile, or your correct postal address so we can pay you by check. If you are a U.S. citizen you will need to fax or mail us a W-9 form.

That's it. You bring us paying members, you get paid.

We took Social Media to a whole new level by offering commissions, and it's another reason why Sokule is Not Your Grandmother's Social Media Site

Chapter 5 – Creating a Business Presence Online...

Many online marketers don't have a home for their business. They don't have a central place they can send people. They just have affiliate link and often send people to others' sites without trying to get them to a website of their own, or get them on a list of their own.

Let me state this clearly. You need an online home for your business, even if you are just an affiliate marketer.

A business home on the internet is basically a central place you send people to get the information they need. Others want to know who you are and how you can help them solve problems they have.

You have probably heard the phrase, "All roads lead to Rome." On the internet, it is "all roads lead to home."

When you are just starting out, you must position yourself as the expert and brand a website, and then funnel your traffic to that website.

So let's show you how to use Sokule to create that much-needed home for your business on the web.

When you first log in to Sokule you will see you have two affiliate links, a general sales link (http://sokule.com/[yourusername]), and a postit link. The postit link looks like – http://sokule.com/postit/[yourusername] – and it's this link we will mainly focus on since this is going to be the new home for your business.

If you are a free member your page will look something like this...

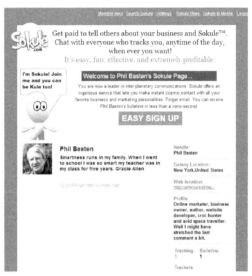

Now this is a start, but it not a business presence yet. It needs a few additions that will make it uniquely me.

It needs some links to sites I like and promote. It needs to tell people what Social Media sites I like and belong to. It needs to have some videos that tell people about a particular product I like or tell them my story.

And it could use some informative posts and maybe a little humor.

After all, we don't want to end up like the boring major in Good Morning, Vietnam who said, "That's humor. I recognize that," do we? :-)

Now my page needs all this but I can't do this as a free member. I need to be a Bronze member and select the add-ons I want, or I need to be a Bronze Plus, Silver, Gold, or Founder member where I get everything.

Now my page might look like this...

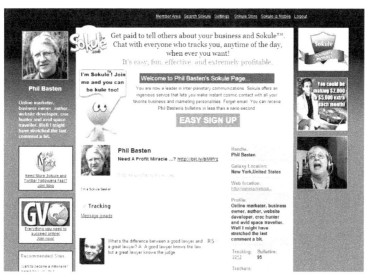

Finally I am getting somewhere. I have the makings of a home on the internet.

You'll notice that I have links to sites I recommend, links to special programs, a graphic ad and a video, and I even have Social Media links further down the page on the left-hand side, along with ClickBank links to give me additional passive income.

If I was really smart, every link I add to this page would eventually lead back to this page so I could create a funnel effect.

Additionally, everything I do online should have one goal: drive traffic to my new business presence online and build my following.

You also notice that there is an easy signup button on my page. Each person who comes to my site, clicks that button, and signs up under me becomes one of my trackers or followers.

That is huge because, as an upgraded member, I can direct squeek (email) all my trackers or followers every three days and it doesn't matter how many people I have following me. There are no restrictions.

Are you starting to see why it is so important to have your own business presence on the Internet?

Adding live links, videos, and graphics to your postit page is something else that is unique to Sokule, which is another reason why it's Not Your Grandmother's Social Media Site.

In the next chapter we are going to show you a great way to grow your trackers or followers and build your list quickly by using something else that is unique to Sokule called Sokens. They are the coins of the realm at Sokule.

One of our founding members, Gabriella Darko, will show you exactly why Sokens are so important at Sokule and how you can put them to work for you.

Chapter 6 – Hey Buddy Can You Spare a Soken...?

By Gabriella DArko - Sokule Founding Member.
http://sokule.com/postit/spark

I have always had a special attraction toward coins. My uncle was a numismatist, and he taught me to love and appreciate coins. One of my first memories is staring at a beautiful claret velvet box and the shiny coin it contained... my very first, very own coin!

It was a real treasure for a two-year old, and it was love at first sight. A love and appreciation has deepened with the years.

No wonder I was excited when Jane announced Sokens— our own Sokule cyber-money. Yes, Sokens are cyber coins, but coins that have very real value.

The Sokens tool is my favorite application at Sokule, and here's why...

First, let me say something that will really shock you...

The money is in your list.

But then you knew that already, right?

And what is the most important task of your Sokens or cyber-coins?

That's right—to help you get more trackers and grow your list.

You will find Sokens in your Sokule members' area. You can't miss them. They are located on the left-hand side in the second set of five boxes. They have an icon that looks like a dartboard with a big blue S on the icon.

But Sokens are much more than cyber-coins. When you click on the Sokens icon you will see a page with these links on it: Earn Sokens, Buy Sokens, Offer Sokens Claim Sokens, Give Sokens...

- You can "buy" new trackers with your Sokens. The larger your bribe, the more trackers or followers you can get.
- Your posts get noticed, read, and rated, because we reward members when they participate.
- You can offer Sokens as a bonus to your trackers to entice them to join your business opportunity or programs, or buy products you promote.
- You can give your Sokens away as...
  (a) Thank you gifts.
  (b) Birthday Gifts—See the birthday application in your members' area.
  (c) "Just because" gifts. Just because you are a generous friend, or you like   doing nice things for others.

How can you earn Sokens?

- When you join Sokule you receive a sign-up bonus of 5,000 to 1 million Sokens, depending on your membership level.
- When you sign up other people you receive a bonus of 25 to 2,500 Sokens depending on your membership level.
- You can buy Sokens. Paid members get huge discounts.
- You collect Bonus Sokens when you join or sign up at certain programs where Sokens are being offered as a bonus. Hint: look for Jane's offers. She is always extremely generous. It's one of the main reasons I read Jane's "Message from the President" every day. :-)
- You can earn between 2 and 100 Sokens by rating other peoples' posts. You'll find little stars under

every post. The more you like the post, the more stars you can give as a rating.
- You receive Sokens when you track new members. Click on "Claim Sokens." You will see a long list of new members. Click on the green "Track" sign on the right, one by one. With this one click two things happen.
(1) You are making a new connection and hopefully they will track you back at some point, and...
(2) You also receive the amount of Sokens that this person has offered for the tracking. Look at the purple box on the upper-right corner of your site. This tells you how many Sokens you have available to use.
- You can earn from 100 to 1,000 random Sokens when you click on member ads or banners.
- Note: You should go to the Sokens application as soon as you sign in to Sokule. Collect every available Soken you can and do it several times a day.

So! You have your Sokens. Now what?

TAKE ACTION!

I know, the high numbers look really nice in your purple box, but this is not meant to be a decoration! It will not raise your prestige. Remember, if money does not move, it is worthless! Sokens are just like the Green Stuff. You are wealthy in direct proportion to the amount of money passing through your hands.

Go to your Sokens application, but this time, click on the "Offer Sokens" link. You should make the highest offer you can. Just keep in mind that you need to have at least ten times the Sokens in your account that your offer, so you will get at least ten new trackers. If you offer 5,000 Sokens for each tracker you must have 50,000 Sokens in your account.

Your goal is to get on the Top 25 list. The higher your offer, the more people will see it, and the more people may choose to track you.

KEEP THOSE SOKENS MOVING!

You'll be happy you did.

Keep in mind, your post will appear on more than forty sites!

Use your Sokens wisely... Make a Soken Bonus offer when you advertise your programs and services, and you'll get Sokule signups at the same time. How kule is that?

Show how kind and thoughtful you are and be sure to check "Whose Birthday is it?" when you first log in. Click the cake at the top of the page.

Our friend, The Gentle Giant, never forgets anyone's birthday. He makes it easy for us to be nice. Click on the "Cake" on your member site, and send your cards. I do it every day. You can even personalize your card, and yes, you can send Gift Sokens with it.

It's easy to make people feel special on their special day at Sokule.

Make others feel special and maybe down the track they will make sure you feel special when they buy stuff from you. Good things have a habit of coming round full circle.

Aren't Sokens the Kulest?

Sokens: they are another good reason why Sokule is Not Your Grandmother's Social Media Site.

Chapter 7 - Trackers and Tracking...

Trackers at Sokule are the same as followers at Twitter, and fans at Facebook.

If I am tracking you it means I am following your posts to see if you have anything interesting to say. Maybe you offer some good advice for me, a tip or two, advance notice about a new launch I might be interested in, or something to brighten my day. If you are tracking me, you are probably looking for something similar.

If I am following your posts, then I am tracking you. If you are following my posts, then I am being tracked by you. Get it?

So how do you and I get people to track us?

The internet functions on the law of reciprocity. Basically, this law says if I do something for you then somewhere down the track you may do something similar for me. How this works in Social Media is I follow you first and at some point you may reciprocate and follow me.

If you want people to track you, be the leader and make the first move. Start following the people you want to have follow you and begin developing those mutual relationships you are looking for.

There are a number of ways to get trackers...

1.   Sokule Sokens (credits)...

Sokens are perhaps the fastest and most popular way to get trackers. The idea here is that you offer Sokens to others as an incentive to get them to track you. The larger your offers, the higher up you appear on the gift list, and the more likely you are to entice others to track you.

To claim the Sokens you are offering, others must track you. It's a simple exchange. They want your Sokens so they can offer Sokens too and entice others to follow them. To see how they work be sure to check out Chapter 6 called, Hey Buddy, Can You Spare a Soken?

Members also want to earn Sokens so they can send a birthday card along with a small gift of Sokens (50 to 100) to each person tracking them whose birthday it is. It's a great way to build relationships.

Just log in to your member's area, click on the 'Sokens' link, and then go to claim Sokens. When you have earned enough Sokens, go to 'Offer Sokens,' make an offer, and members will start tracking you.

Don't have time to spend earning Sokens credits? No worries, you can always purchase them, make your offer, and go about doing other things until your next post.

2.   You can search for people you want to track...

To do this you simply log in to your account, go to your members' area, scroll down, and click on the 'Search Users' icon.

You can search for people with similar interests as you by selecting 'Search by Category.' You can even search for people in certain countries you wish to follow.

You can search for people by type (e.g., online marketer, offline business, home-based business). You can even search for people by username, last name, or a phrase you saw in one of their posts.

3.   **Suggested users...**

Another way you can get more people to track you is to use the suggested users' tool. Just click the link at the top of the page when you get to the search page.
This will bring up a list of people you are not tracking yet. You can "select all" if you are in a hurry, or you can select a few—twenty to thirty—and wait and see how many follow you, before you move to the next batch.

For example, If you want to follow all or some of the members who are interested in music at Sokule, just select the category "music" from the drop-down menu at the search function. Click on the ones you want to track or click "track all" and you will have access to all the music lovers at Sokule. I am one of them. :-)

4.   **Thanks for the track messages...**

If you left the notices checked in your settings, you will receive 'Thanks for the Track' emails when others start tracking you.

To track them, you simply click on the user name in the email of the person tracking you. This will take you to their postit page when you should see a green button that says "Track Me" or white button that says "Tracking," and that means you are already tracking this person.

The reason that you want to track those that are tracking you is a matter of retention. You want to keep as many trackers as you can. Trackers = Money. The more trackers you have, the more money you can make. Your trackers are your list. You want to build it and retain it.

Some people get ticked off when they track you and you don't reciprocate. If they stop tracking you your numbers may diminish, and that is not the result you are looking for.

Sokule gives you many unique ways to find people and track them, and this is another reason why it's not your Grandmother's Social Media site.

Chapter 8 - Posting on Sokule, the Long and Short of It...

Posting is easy at Sokule and it is extremely powerful.

There are basically four kinds of posts you can do.

*   A short post of 140 characters. Just enough to whet your readers' appetites.

*   A medium-length post of 500 characters. Perfect for when you have something important to say.

*   An article-length or as-long-as-you-like post on Sokwall, and...

*   A welcome post to all members on Kule Wall.

When you log in to Sokule, the first thing you will see is Kule Wall. This is one of our posting walls on Sokule. These are posts made by our paying members.

If you are new to Sokule, read some of these posts by our paying members and examine what they are doing. You will not be able to post on Kule Wall unless you are a Bronze Plus member or above, so if you are a free member, just hit "Continue to Members' Area" at the bottom of the post.

Here is what Kule Wall looks like. You will see five posts and at the bottom it will say "Continue to Members' Area."

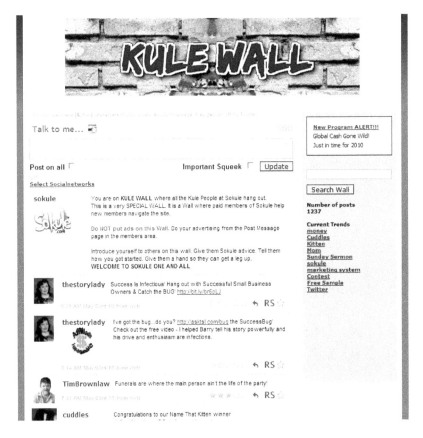

Assuming you just clicked "Continue to Members' Area," you should now find yourself looking at the members' control page. This page has a series of icons on it. Each icon will lead you to a specific function.

Don't panic. We will go through each one of these for you in this reference guide.

The first and most important box that you are going to see says "Post Message."

This is the box you want to go to get your message out on Sokule. Here you can post a message of 140 characters.

When you post your message you are going to see this...

If you want to just post on Sokule for your trackers to see, you simply pop in your message, hit the update button, wait a few seconds, and bingo! That's it. Your message should now appear on your post message page and on your own postit page so your followers (trackers) can see it.

Now suppose you want your Sokule post to appear on your Twitter account.

Click on the Blue Bird Icon on the right-hand side, fifth row of boxes. When you see the popup, click NO and continue to the next page.

Always click NO when you see this popup. You want to see both the secure sections and the images on the page.

Next Click – Add Network

Then enter your Twitter username and password in the marked fields and click the save button.

When you make a post at Sokule, click on the check box that says "Post on All" and then click "update" so your post appears on Sokule and Twitter instantly...

Once you click "update," your post will appear on Sokule and on Twitter instantly. It's really kule. Go to your Twitter account right after you post at Sokule and check it out.

Of course, there's a lot more you can do with a post if you are an upgraded member. If you are Bronze or above at Sokule, the posting box will open up and it will let you post a message up to 500 characters long.

Upgrade to Bronze Plus or higher and a whole world of posting opens up to you.

You can make article-length posts at Sokwall. (See chapter 12 on Sokwall.)

The Sokwall icon can be found on the first row of the members' control page. It looks like this...

| Post Message | Sokule Stars | Upgrade Today | Social Media Posting Sites | Post On Sokwall |

Click on the icon and you will come to a page like this...

Post this on other my Socialnetworks...

Post on all ☐   Select Socialnetworks

Allow post to ping additional weblogs ☐

Post on kulewall ☐

Talk to me...

Tell me more...

B *I* <u>U</u> ABC | ≣ ≣ ≣ ≣ | – Styles – ∨ | – Format – ∨ | – Font family – ∨ | – Font size – ∨

✂ 🔏 📋 📄 🗐 | 🔍 🔤 | ⦂☰ ☰ | 🔲 🔲 | ↻ ↺ | ∞ 💥 🔗 ⚓ 🖉 | HTML | **A** ⏷ ✏ ⏷

📝 | ▣ ▣ | ⦂ ⦂ ⦂ | ⁿ ₙ ⦂ | 🔲 🔲 | — ⦸ 🔲 | x₂ x² | Ω | ¶ ¶ | 🔣 ↺ 🔍

Path:

Add Video...

Embed Tags   URL Source File

Just paste your \<embed\> \<img\> or \<object\> tags below Use this for videos & widgets

Where do you want to show your media? ⦿ above the text | ○ below the text

Save Post

The first thing you should take notice of is that there is an editor where you can customize your post. You can add a video or graphic to your post. You can highlight certain keywords or phrases in your posts.

Sokwall lets you post a full promo or an article-length message. You can add images to your posts. You can Re-Squeek and Re-Tweet your posts. You can add your posts to Kule Wall, which is the first set of posts people see when they log in.

Sokule gives you enormous flexibility in the way you can customize your posts and make them stand out from the crowd so you get noticed.
How can Sokule post messages that are as long as a tigers' tale and still have those posts appear on other sites like Twitter, FaceBook, MySpace, and thirty-five other sites where the post length is limited?

Is it Magic?

Not really. Here is how we do it.

When you make a longer post, Sokule inserts a bit.ly link so that people reading your posts at Twitter or FaceBook will see the first 120 characters of your post and the bit.ly link.

When they click on that bit.ly link, it will lead them back to your full post. So make sure the first 120 characters are targeted and strong enough to entice people to click your bit.ly link. After all, you want them to read your entire post, right?

Sokule was created so you can advertise your business quickly and easily to a continually expanding audience online.

Post 140 characters.
Post 500 characters.
Or post article-length messages.
You choose the way you want your posts to appear and how long you want them to be.

Sokule is not your one-size-fits-all Social Media site. We made it so you can make posts that reflect your own personality which is another Kule reason why it's not your grandmother's Social Media site.

Chapter 9 – Our Posting Sites Help You Brand Yourself...

If you have just joined Sokule recently, you may have noticed that you can now post to more than forty top Social Media sites and blogs. At least, it was slightly more than forty at the time of the writing of this book. :-)

More than forty sites is a lot. At Sokule, you can get mass exposure for your business. We are always looking out for posting sites and will add more when we find suitable ones. This is a never-ending quest at Sokule.

You'll find the Social Media sites you can post to in your Sokule members' control panel in the first row. The graphic below shows the section of the members' control page we are talking about.

When you click the Social Media sites link or icon you will see a message popup that says, "Do you want to view only the webpage content that was delivered securely?" and here you want to click NO because you want to view all content, including images.

After you click NO you will come to a page with a collection of popular Social Media sites on it...

Social Networking Posting Site

Twitter	Edit Network	Blogger	Edit Network
Live Journal	Edit Network	Delicious	Edit Network
Posterous	Edit Network	WordPress	Edit Network
FriendFeed	Edit Network	YouAre	Edit Network
Diigo	Edit Network	Koornk	Edit Network
Plurk	Edit Network	Multiply	Edit Network

At the time of writing this book, there were more than forty Social Media sites and blogs that Sokule posts to.

- Twitter (3 accounts)
- FaceBook
- MySpace
- Blogger
- Word Press
- Delicious
- Yahoo Profiles
- Live Journal
- Posterous
- Plurk
- FriendFeed
- You Are
- FaceBook Pages
- Vox
- Qaiku
- Diigo
- Koornk
- Multiply
- Tumblr
- Jaiku
- Utterli
- ShoutEm
- Brightkite
- Typepad
- Radar
- Friendster
- Present.ly
- Windows Live
- Hyves
- Pikchur

- Numpa
- Apsense
- Sonico

- Pixelpipe
- Zannel
- Twitxr

These sites are available as an add-on, which free members can purchase for $29.95 a month. Bronze members can add them for $14.95 a month, or they are free with our Bronze Plus, Silver, Gold, and Founder memberships.

It's an impressive list, right? But, if you're anything like me, the thought of having to join each of these sites, upload your picture, add your profile, add your website links, and then add your login info for each one into Sokule seems like a daunting task, right?
You're probably thinking, "I know it will be worth it in the end but do I really have to set up my profile in each of the sites more than forty times?"

We'll, yes you do. You may long for the ice cream dessert but you have to get through the main meal first.

But there is an answer. Maybe you don't have to do this yourself, after all...

Read on to find out about a really kule service we created with our partners.

But before we do that, let me show you exactly what you need to do at each of the posting sites, and we'll use Diigo as an example.

So let's set up Diigo. First, I need to enter my profile information.

diigo
ve.6 beta

Research, Share, Collaborate

My Library   My Network   My Groups   Community

Phil Basten   Message   Frier

🏠 / My Profile / Edit

Edit My Profile   Preview

Basic   Interests   Privacy   Me elsewhere   Picture

Name: First name: Phil   Last name: Basten

About Me: Online marketer, business owner, author, website developer, croc hunter and avid space traveller. Well I might have stretched the last comment a bit.

(Max 300 characters)   🔒 Anyone

I use Diigo because: It easy and fun to use, I can reach my business associates. I can expand my network and run group discussions.

(Max 300 characters. Share how you use Diigo.)   🔒 Diigo Users

Connect with others practicing in the same field as you   🔒 Diigo Users

Industry: Marketing and Advertising ▾

Provide us with your location, so you can easily connect with users near you   🔒 Diigo Users

Country: United States ▾

Region: New York

Zip / Postal Code: 10003

(Max 300 characters. Share how you use Diigo.)   🔒 Diigo Users

Connect with others practicing in the same field as you   🔒 Diigo Users

Industry: Marketing and Advertising ▾

Provide us with your location, so you can easily connect with users near you   🔒 Diigo Users

Country: United States ▾

Region: New York

Zip / Postal Code: 10003

City: New York

Your language preferences will help us recommend content and people to you   🔒 Diigo Users

Primary Language: English ▾

Second Language: ---- ▾

Third Language: ▾

Save Changes   Cancel

As you can see, there is a bunch of information I need to add.

Next I need to add my picture, make sure that it is 120x120 pixels square, and ensure that it's a close-up shot of my face if I want it to look right. People like to see who they are dealing with.

So this took about five minutes to do. Some sites ask for similar amounts of information, some sites ask for less. The point is it takes time to set your profile up in each site. But it's well worth the effort.

The other point you need to consider is that when you set up a profile in each of the sites, you should use the same username and info in each one so you brand yourself on the internet. But this presents another issue. You'll need to do some searches to see if the username is available or if someone is already using it.

If this seems like a lot of work to do, we've created a service that will do all the setup for you. That's right, our partners will do it all for you. You simply pay for the service, fill in a form, and enter all your information, one time, and they will...

- Join each of the more than forty sites for you, or just the ones you are not a member of yet,
- Set up the profiles for you in each site with your brand or username, and
- Enter all this information into Sokule for you.

All you need to do is add a post and click, send, and your message will go to all top Social Media posting sites. How easy is that?

To access this service, log in to your members' area, go to the first set of boxes on the control page, click on the social networks icon, and follow the instructions.

If you are in a hurry you can click this link and access the service directly.
http://linktrack.info/profiles_done_for_you

Make sure you have all your information saved in notepad, and you have your picture ready before you pay for the service. You will need this information close by when you fill in the form.

Sokule was built for business people who need an instant presence on the internet, which is why it's Not Your Grandmother's Social Media Site.

Chapter 10 – Pre-schedule – Make Posting Easy...

By Kathy Pleasance, Sokule, Founding Member.
http://sokule.com/postit/kthlp

Schedule Posts is one of the many tools that moved Sokule ahead of the pack. This is a 'Must Do' feature which you should not overlook.

This tool gives you the power to be a professional with minimal effort and it's an easy way to make Social Media work for you.

You should be posting several times a day, every day. Exposure matters. A constant presence on the internet is vital to becoming a successful Internet Marketer.

The problem for most people is that they have limited time to spend in front of their computers. For many people it is virtually impossible to post every day. The solution – schedule your posts! You need to work smart, not hard.

With the Schedule Posts tool you can schedule up to twenty-five squeeks or posts in advance. I find the best way is to organize my work routine to schedule squeeks for the upcoming week on a Monday morning.

The other thing I like to do is to make sure that there are always a few squeeks sitting in the queue. I hate having to rush and get them done at the last moment.

I especially load up before going on holidays so no one will miss me! Even if I am away for a week, Sokule will be working hard for me while I am taking that well-deserved vacation.

Scheduled Posts can found in the Applications for: Bronze Plus, Silver, Gold, and Founding members at the bottom of the members' control page, and here is how they work.

Post on All...

When you get to the "Pre-schedule Squeeks" box, make sure you check the "Post on all" box so your pre-scheduled posts will go out to more than forty Social Media sites.

Make it a habit to check this box before you start posting...

In fact, I suggest you go directly to "Post on all" and check this icon before you do anything else. If you are like me, you will forget to check it and your scheduled post will not go out to all your Social Media sites.

If you haven't joined all the social sites yet, then take the time to do this. It's really important. The time that you will save by posting to all sites, at one time, and the exposure that you will gain, is priceless. You want to take full advantage of this awesome Sokule feature.

Select Social Networks...

If you wish certain posts to be displayed only on certain targeted sites, you can do that too. Just make this selection first, before entering your squeek. Again, I'd make it a habit to select all social sites as soon as you land on this page.

Talk To Me...

Talk to me...

Scheduled Date: Scheduled Hours: Scheduled Minutes:
                       Hrs ⌄   Mins ⌄   Update

"Talk to me" is where you enter your message. You can post messages or squeeks up to 500 characters long. As you enter your message, the 500 counter displayed on the right will decrease. When this counter reaches zero, that's it, you're done.

You will not be able to enter any more data.

Your 500 characters include any link you enter in your post, so make sure you leave room for that after your text.

Keep an eye on the counter to make sure that you can end your message before you reach the maximum allowable size.

Writing tips...

Use a link tracker to track your click thru rate. You can get a good one here - http://bit.ly/linktrack

• Make your posts interesting. I find a little humor goes a long way.
• Do not just promote your product—post informative facts relating to your business.
• Post on things you are passionate about.
• Create your own personality so that people will look forward to reading your next post or squeek. If you just post adverts, you will quickly lose your trackers' interest and give them little reason to continue following you.

Scheduled Date...

To schedule a date, click inside the blank white box under the words "Schedule Date" to display the current month's calendar. You will see that today's date is highlighted.

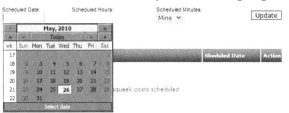

Then you just need to click on the desired year, month, or day for the date to appear in the white box. You have just set your date. It's easier than you think!

To change the selected date, simply click inside the white box again.

Scheduled Hour, Scheduled Minutes...

Schedule your squeek posts according to our current server time. Our servers are located in Texas, USA.

Current Server Date & Time : **2010-06-01 12:06:11** (Central Daylight Time (CDT) -0500 UTC)

If you want to know what day and time it is where our servers are - <u>click here</u>

Make sure your posts are scheduled at least 15 minutes after the current server time, or they will not go out.

Example; you cannot send something yesterday, it's already gone :-)

The "Schedule Squeek" tool displays the current Server Date & Time: 2010-04-13 09:24:00. This is (Central Daylight Time (CDT) -0500 UTC).

Current Server Date & Time Translates To: year/month/day hour/minutes/sec. The Time Zone in which the Sokule server resides is Central US.

Sokule will not do 'the time warp' into the past to post your squeek. Yesterday is gone. In fact—your post must be at least fifteen minutes ahead of the current server time. This is to allow the server cron-jobs enough time to pick up your squeek and place them in the queue ahead of the server time.

Be aware—the date/time displayed is not interactive; it does not change. If you have taken thirty minutes to create your squeek, the minutes displayed will now be thirty minutes behind.

Make it a rule to post several hours ahead of the hour displayed, to ensure that you are well ahead of the actual server time. If the hours and minutes are critical to your post, then check the current server time with the link provided.

http://www.worldtimeserver.com/current_time_in_US-NY.aspx

Click the down arrow for both the Scheduled Hour and Minutes and make a selection that is well ahead of the current time. A valid hour and minute must be selected before Update is allowed.

Be careful when scheduling a post to the exact hour and minute to correspond to the launch time of a new product or site. Always check what time zone that launch is in, then compare it to the Central Time Zone. Make sure that you adjusted the time accordingly.

If you post after the launch, you will have missed a window of opportunity, and posting early just spells disaster.

Update...

Double check your work—once you update it you will NOT be able to modify your message.

I personally use the Scheduled Squeeks feature every week. It allows me the freedom I need to concentrate on other aspects of my business.

The time that I save, along with the level of professionalism that I have achieved, goes well beyond the "Wow Factor."

Thank you, Jane and Phil, for creating Sokule and allowing me to part of such an awesome site.

To learn more about Kathy Pleasance, go here...
http://sokule.com/postit/kthlp

Kathy schedules her posts in advance, and this is another great reason why Sokule is Not Your Grandmother's Social Media Site.

Chapter 11 - Learning the Lingo...

Sokule has a rich language all its own. It's fun to learn and even more fun to use.

For example:

- When you make a post at Sokule it's called a Squeek.
- You can re-squeek at Sokule, which is like a re-tweet at Twitter.
- Sokule lets you re-tweet your message at Twitter and re-squeek it at Sokule at the same time, which is really nifty.
- You can become a Sokule Star by getting 1,000 members or more to track you. When you do, your postit affiliate page receives three flashing gold stars and you become a Sokule Seeker.
- When you get 5,000 trackers or more, you become a Sokule Achiever and you receive four gold flashing stars.
- When you get 10,000 trackers or more, you become a Sokule Master and you receive five gold flashing stars.
- If someone follows you at Sokule, they are called trackers.
- When you follow someone at Sokule, you are tracking them.
- A Squeekie is someone who is brand new to Sokule and,

... Here's my favorite...

- A user who drinks when they post is called a Squeekeasy.

Every now and then our members come up with some humdingers to add to the Sokule Lingo chart.

If you want to see all of the current Sokule Lingo, go to... http://www.sokule.com/lingo.html

People have asked us why it's important to have a Sokule Lingo section. Sokule is a Social Media advertising site. It interacts with people in a fun and interesting way and it is part of what makes Social Media sites popular.

Sokule keeps people smiling and Sokule Lingo is just part of the whole picture.

We have a Sokule Store where people can actually wear Sokule on their backs. I do this all the time and it is a great way to advertise Sokule.

People often stop my partner, Phil, and me in the street to ask what Sokule is and it is a great way to start a conversation when you are out on the town or shopping at the local mall.

New additions and innovations...

Part of what makes Sokule unique are the constant innovation and changes we make to the site to keep it fresh and interesting for our members. Hardly a week goes by where we do not add some new feature to Sokule. When we do, we update the lingo page to reflect those new applications so our members are kept in the loop.

For example, we have two very Kule Walls at Sokule. One was added recently! As soon as it was ready we added it to the Sokule Lingo section.

In the next chapter, you will find out about those Walls at Sokule, and no, it has nothing to do with climbing the wall...

Chapter 12 – Climbing the Walls – Sokwall & Kule Wall...

By Nina Spelman - Sokule Founding Member.
http://sokule.com/postit/jkspel

Do you read all your email? I certainly don't. My mailbox can get 300 to 500 emails in it while I am sleeping. Most of those emails are heading for the trash can, and how often do they end up in SPAM? Much too often!

And what about the hours spent 'clicking' for credits—just way too many to admit. HA! Who are we kidding? Hours and hours to get one click on our link! It's embarrassing, and it certainly won't 'make you rich' in twenty-four hours or less.

Social Media is the future of Internet Marketing. These Social Media networks are quickly replacing the opt-in mailing list. We are not there yet, but with the magic of SOKWALL, it could happen before you know it.

Enter the MAGIC of SOKWALL!

Bronze Plus, Silver, Gold, and Founder members can use SOKWALL as part of their memberships. If you are not an upgraded member, you can purchase a SOKWALL for $5.00 per month. It's a great investment.

With one SOKWALL Post, your ad has hit thirty-three different WEBLOGS, hit more than forty different Social

Networks, and posted to the 'Spread the Word' page of on the hottest Social Network site today—SOKULE.

With one click, your ad is EVERYWHERE and everyone is reading it!! That one SOKWALL post is now worth its weight in GOLD and countless hours of your time.

Your SOKWALL post can have a video, a banner, a lovely picture, your picture, clickable links, or whatever you want to add.

Do you have an inspiring idea or review that you want to share? A blog is a great place and Sokwall functions much like a blog except that it is much easier and faster to maneuver around it.

How to make magic...

Step 1: Select your favorite Social Network:

Notice this box:

Post this on other my Socialnetworks...
    Post on all ☐   Select Socialnetworks
Allow post to ping additional weblogs ☐
Post on kulewall ☐

This is where the magic starts.

Post this on other my Social Networks

You can do two things here...

- **Post on all**: just click on the box. This will place your ad out to thirty-eight social networks. You must be a member of each one.

Post on all ☑

Or...

- You can simply click – **Select Social Networks** – and chose the networks you want your post to appear on. They will appear like this...

Click on the little box if you are a member of that social network. If you are not sure, click on the little icon and create an account. Remember, your ad will be posted to each Social Network that you are a member of.

Make sure you ping the additional weblogs...

Allow post to ping additional weblogs

Hover over the little box that says "Allow post to ping additional weblogs." What drops down is a list of all the WEBLOGS your post will be sent to.

A weblog often is a "log of our times" from a particular point-of-view.

Generally, weblogs are devoted to one or several subjects or themes, usually of topical interest, and can be thought of as developing commentaries, individual or collective on their particular themes.

A weblog may consist of the recorded ideas of an individual (a sort of diary), or be a complex collaboration open to anyone. Most of the latter are moderated discussions.

Search engines (Google, MSN, Yahoo, etc...) crawl the weblogs daily looking for keyword identification and new content. If your ad or article is full of high quality keywords, and interesting content, the search engines are much more likely to pick it up and rank it highly.

Another important aspect of SOKWALL, compared to article submission or an email campaign, is the fact that SOKWALLs can be 'Edited'. This is huge! You can 'tweak' your SOKWALL until it is full of the right high-quality keywords that will rank higher in the search engines.

Because of the power of Sokwall, I rarely use the short posting box at Sokule anymore. I can make my post as long or as short as I like, so why use the "post message " box when I can do everything I want at Sokwall all day long?

Post on Kule Wall from Sokwall.

If you are a Bronze Plus member or higher, your post will not only be posted on the Sokule 'Spread the Word' page, but you can also post on Kule Wall.

Kule Wall is the first page all Sokule members see when they log into Sokule. A post there is visible to all members, and not just your personal trackers.

Kule Wall is seen by all members of Sokule and, shortly, we will be expanding to other networks to increase the audience who will see your posts.

To make a post to Kule Wall, simply check the box that says "Post on Kule Wall."

Post on kulewall ⌐

Just keep in mind you can only post quality information, events, helpful advice, answer questions about Sokule, and so on. No ads are allowed on Kulewall. This is where you get noticed as a resident Sokule expert and you can build your credibility and reputation fast if you do it right.

Step 1. Give your post a title...

Talk to me...

Your title is the most important part of your Sokwall post. If people do not find your title interesting or of benefit to them, they probably will not click on it when they visit other networks, and that means they won't read the rest of your post.

The job of your title is to capture people's attention and interest and make them want to read more.

Step 2. Tell me more...

This is the body of your ad or article. This is where you will place your links, videos, music, pictures, or whatever you can think that will empower your ad or article. Fill it with high-quality, highly searched keywords...

Just a few tips:

1. HTML: Look above and find HTML (third from the right)

When you click on this link, a box will pop up with your ad in HTML code.

So this: 'Join Sokule Today' will look like this in HTML code... <p> </p><p>Join SOKULE today </ p><p> </p>

A bunch of gobbled gook, right? But Sokule converts it into readable text before it sends your message out. You will see it change to text right before your eyes when you hit save.

2. Insert hyperlink...

With this symbol ∾ you can turn your website link into a 'CLICKABLE' URL. All you need to do is highlight your website link, then click on the chain (link) symbol. When you do, this box will pop up...

You can make your link clickable, make it open in a new window, or even add a title (sales phrase) that people will see when they mouse over your website link.

This will make your website link look like this http://sokule.com/jkspel
Or, you could turn Join SOKULE Today into Join SOKULE Today

Step 3. Add Video...

There is one more thing you can do to enhance your posts and make them stand out. You can add an image, a widget, an audio, or a video.

Where do you want to show your media?

You can choose "above the text" or "below the text." When your POST is ready, simply hit the "SAVE POST," and Congratulations! You just wrote on your SOKWALL!

SOKWALL will now take your post and transform your masterpiece into short line with a bit-ly URL, which can now be added to any article, blog, and Social Media site or email campaign.

BIT-LY shortens those long affiliate URLs and makes them perfect for Twitter, Facebook, and all the other Social Media sites.

Let's face it... Social Media is the future of Internet Marketing. Don't fight it, get prepared. You will want to be ahead of the pack!

KULE WALL is where you can meet the smartest marketers in the world. They are on SOKULE and they have done the math. They are the BRONZE plus, SILVER, GOLD, and FOUNDER members of SOKULE who have figured out that dollar for dollar, an upgraded membership in SOKULE gets the best advertising on the net.

FOUNDERS can post three times a day, Gold and Silver can post twice a day, and Bronze plus are allowed one post a day. These posts can speak volumes!

KULE WALL highlights these brilliant marketers and gives you a chance to meet them, learn from them, and get a glimpse of who they are.

They will reveal their inspirations and secrets to their success.

Kule Wall is NOT for ADS! ADS belong on the SPREAD the WORD page.

Kule Wall is for introductions, tips, event announcements, and a place to get your questions answered. It is a place where you can learn from the experiences of those who have built small empires and apply what you learn to your own business.

Inspirations of success!
- Learn from Kule Wall
- Grow with Kule Wall
- Inspire and be inspired
- This is KULE WALL!

Sokule is unique and stands head and shoulders above other sites. It offers you a way to get a real message of any length all over the net.

The two walls at Sokule, Sokwall and Kule Wall, do not exist anywhere else on the net, which is why Sokule is Not Your Grandmother's Social Media Site.
Nina Spelman
@jkspel at SOKULE
http://sokule.com/postit/jkspel

Chapter 13 - Make Your Posts Count...

There is a right way and a wrong way to post on Sokule, or any other Social Media site for that matter.

The one thing you need to keep in mind when you are at a Social Media site is that people do not like to be peppered by ads.

- Your trackers want information, not ads. Peppering people with ads all the time is like going to a department store and having the sales people jump all over you as soon as you set foot through the door. You and I don't like that. Don't come across that way to others. They will stop following you.
- People want to know who you are, what you do, and what is working for you. Give them good, solid reviews of products and services you have tried and tell them which ones worked for you or made some money for you. They'll respect you for it.
- People want to see your picture so they know they are dealing with a real person and not a virtual assistant. I much prefer to deal with a real person with a real picture so I can see what they look like. Do not put up a picture of a cat, even if it is cute as a button, unless you are selling cat supplies or you meow when someone puts a glass of milk in front of you.
- People like to read about what you are doing and who you are doing it with, although I wouldn't go too far with that one :-)

- People want to laugh. Some people are trying hard to make a little money online to supplement an income, or get some money after being laid off, and their daily lives are stressful. Give them something to feel good about, something to laugh at. They will thank you for it.

- People have all kinds of challenges in life. The reason that Social Media sites are so popular now is many people gather together in groups to feel connected and not so alone. They want inspiration. They want to know they are special, that they can achieve their goals and that they matter. If you want to feel inspired yourself, be the inspiration to others.

- People want experts to teach them. Many experts are giving people and are more than willing to help when they have some time. When they do, be thankful and appreciative. It will endear you to people. If there are no experts in your group, or team of followers, become the expert yourself. You can find the answers your people are looking for by searching at Google.

You can be all of these things at a Social Media site if you stop and think about what you are posting. If it is something that would make YOU stop and read it, do it and keep doing it.

If your own posts bore you, or offer others little more than hype and a link, you are cheating them and yourself, and you are limiting your own results. You might want to rethink your strategy and post things that are useful and informative, or solve problems your trackers have.

Sometimes saying nothing at all is wiser, and more productive, than shooting off a post that no one wants to read. If you continue down that road, you may see your trackers leave and start following someone else. This is not what you want. If you are not in the list-building business then you are not going to build a solid business that will be alive and growing in the years to come.

Social Media sites offer you an opportunity to build a list with long-lasting relationships that will grow your business, but if you pepper them with ads, you are shooting yourself in the foot because when you really have something you think would interest your trackers and that you could make some sales with, you lost them already in a maze of useless, boring posts.

Here—let me show you what I mean...

The good, the bad, and the ugly...

The good...

Here is something I posted today at Sokule...

Need a good laugh? Listen in as a bunch of gurus make fools of themselves. Check out the Joe and Mable Show. I warn you; don't listen and drink coffee at the same time. :-) No Boring people allowed here: http://joeandmable.com

I clicked on this just because it really stood out from the crowd.

Watch "Laser Tattoo Removal" http://www.tatoo removal – If you are into Tattoos (which I am not), it is certainly something you might open. It made me open it even though I am not a tattoo freak.

... and here is a really interesting post that one of our Founding members, Peter Watson (Surgreen), made on Kule Wall about Sokwall (see chapter on the Walls). This was useful information that Sokule members can use.

SokWall's ~ luv 'em!

Link to 'em, they can pre-sell a '4 credits' surfer and get 'em to click thru... they also advertise Sokule 4 you simultaneously... your recent Sokwall's are displayed to the side aka MORE exposure of your links.. You can make REALLY BIG squeeks... to my knowledge they do not 'break' affiliate links (more on this ~ need a Sokwall 4 that one!) ~ Are you getting the idea that Sokwall's alone are a VERY good reason to be here! ... Laterz :-).

You can bet Peter is going to get people tracking him from that post because he is offering useful information to everyone who logs into Sokule and his post is friendly and inviting.

This is the kind of post you want to make, particularly when you are using our most visible wall at Sokule which is Kule Wall.

The bad...

I could have said something like – Join my site FREE and make money.

http://joeandmable.com – But everyone says that.

The ugly...

... or this one that I selected on my post message page...

GET PAID - http://xycsite.com

Duh! Everyone says that. It is not likely that I will click on that one.

Here's the point...

Your goal at Sokule is get people to track you. You are building a list of prospects. These are the people you want to develop a relationship with so that when you make a recommendation to them they buy from you. They know who you are. You have established yourself as an expert and built credibility with them. They trust your opinion on things and like you...

We tend to buy from people we know, like, and trust.

So the moral of the story here is...

Think before you post and make your posts count.
Fill them with fun, with interest, or with information, and as you do this you will find that your sales will increase.

It really is worth doing this. The payoff can be huge.

You will learn a lot about business and how to conduct it effectively when you are a Sokule member. You will learn from me. You will learn from my partner, Phil Basten, and, more importantly, you will learn from our very talented Sokule community that Sokule is Not Your Grandmother's Social Media Site.

Chapter 14 - Partner Up...

Sokule has some great partner sites. These are sites that have relevancy and synergy with Sokule. They can create an additional stream of income for you no matter what product you are selling online.

You will find these partner sites in the members' area at the bottom of the page under "partner sites" where it says Partner IDs.

Partner Sites

Partner Sites   Add Partner IDs

Sokule Store

There are four partner sites. I am not going to go into what each one does here. You can read about them on the site.

But here is what is really neat about them: if you like one of them, or all of them, you can add their logos right on your postit page of Sokule with your affiliate link for that program.

Let me show you what I mean...

Here is my postit page...

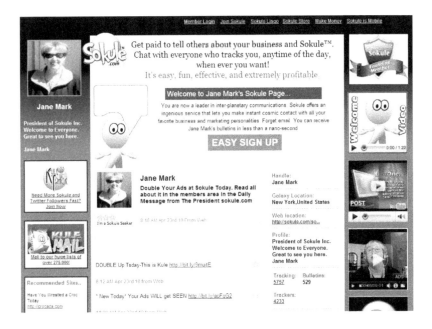

Look at the two logos (Kule Track and Kule Mail) on the left-hand side of my postit page under my picture and bio.

Both of these sites are related to Sokule, so I popped their logos on my postit page, and if someone clicks through to either of those sites while they are on my postit page, I get the sign up or the sale.

The key to being successful online is to send people to a central page, like the one above, and have multiple ways to earn income from it.

Sokule is a Social Media site that expands your earning ability in many ways. You will not find this at most sites, which is why Sokule is Not Your Grandmother's Social Media Site.

Chapter 15 – Become a Spy! Use Keyword Alert...

If you don't know what your competitors are doing, what others are saying about you, or what people are saying about your product or service, your business will quickly become little more than a fading memory. You must know what others are saying and doing to stay ahead of the pack.

Small businesses that do well online find new ways to showcase their wares and new ways to excite people through websites, emails, articles, and public relations copy.

Sokule has you covered with Keyword Alert.

• The first thing you need to do is enter each keyword or key phrase on a new line by clicking "enter" on your keyboard. You can enter up to fifty different words and phrases, but these should be entered one at a time. Keep in mind that you will receive all the keyword results in one digest email. It could be a long email :-)

Most of the time ten or twenty words or phrases should be plenty.

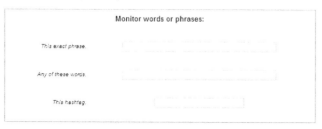

- If you enter the phrase work at home, we will monitor squeeks and tweets that contain the words "work," "at," and "home" in any sequence in the squeek or tweet. That means our report will include entries like "that was hard work," "at my desk," and "the new home is awesome."
- If you enter "work at home" and you want to search on the whole term, leave the quotes around it and we will only monitor squeeks and tweets that contain the entire phrase "work at home." It will also include entries like "work at home opportunity," and "work at home jobs."
- In many cases, basic single keywords will do the job you are looking for, but you can also use our advanced search tool to build more complex keyword phrases. We strongly suggest that you use this tool for anything longer than a simple one-word search, so that your keyword phrase is formatted correctly.

  To ensure you get these alerts in your email account, be sure to white-list admin@sokule.com in your email program or service.
- You can monitor people's comments, attitudes, the area they live in, and topics or themes.

Monitor comments:		Monitor attitudes:	
By this person:		Positive: ☐	
To this person:		Negative: ☐	
About this person:		Asking questions: ☐	

- If, for some reason, you do not receive our email alerts you can always log in to your account and see the latest alert by clicking on "Today's results that we emailed to you."

Results...

Today's results that we emailed to you

You will see a page like this...

- Now what's really powerful is that Keyword Alert monitors your keywords on both Sokule and Twitter. How kule is that?
- But here is the part I love. See the Featured Sokule Member post at the top of the page? That is a member who purchased that position. It has high visibility. It is seen in rotation by members who receive these alerts in their email accounts, when they log in to their accounts to view the alerts online, and it appears on the login page.

- If you'd like high visibility for your site, log in to your account and click on the icon that says "advertise on Sokule," and then click on "Featured bio ad" (Keyword Alert emails). We'll add your entry to the rotation.

- Finally, Keyword Alert allows you to see which keywords or phrases you are tracking, and your stats so you know which ones are working and which ones can be removed or replaced.

Keyword Alert is a powerful tool if you use it properly...

... it lets you receive information from both Twitter and Sokule at the same time.

No other Social Media site provides you with this service, which is why Sokule is Not Your Grandmother's Social Media Site.

Chapter 16 – ReSqueek or ReTweet? – Why Not Do Both...?

If you want to get your message spread virally by others, make it memorable and use the re-squeek, re-tweet tool. It is extremely powerful when used right.

You need to have your own website or blog, and you need to be an upgraded member of Sokule to use this tool; however, if you can create a compelling message that people really like, it could be seen by thousands in just a few days.

So let's find out how to set up this amazing tool up and get your own viral advertising working for you...

Log in to your account and go to the bottom of the control page, then click on the "Get ReSqueek Button" icon. It's the one with the red and the green arrows.

Earnings   Downline   Tracking   Tracked By   Get Resqueek Button

When you click that icon you will be taken to this page...

Manage Resqueek Buttons

Generate New

Sr. No.	Squeek	Resqueeked	Retweeted	Added Date	Action
1	Give your visitors an easy way to pass your me...	1	2	2009-12-15	
2	I just found a great way to spread my message ...	9	6	2009-12-14	
3	Heres a great way to spread your message viral...	4	2	2009-12-14	

Here, you can set up your ReSqueek and ReTweet buttons. In the picture above you can see that I have set up three re-squeek / re-tweet buttons.

So click on "Generate New" and let me show you how to set up a Re-squeek Button for your website!

Step 1 – Add a re-squeek button...

write your message here (Required):

Char Limit: 180

Here is where you write the message you want others to re-squeek or re-tweet.

Here are a few tips to help you...

• Be creative... Ask yourself, "what would make me want to pass this on to people I know? Is it news worthy, important, funny, weird, time sensitive, controversial?"
• Be brief... Get straight to the point. You only have 180 characters to work with so don't waffle on.
• Have a call to action – register here, sign up here, free to join, register free, sign up free, no credit card required, download free now.

If you entered an event notice, you are going to want to send people somewhere to sign up, so in the next field enter the link you want them to go to.

append link to message (Optional):

Lastly, you need to enter the link to the website these buttons will be displayed on. This is for Sokule company use only. No one else sees this link or information.

URL of web page where you will use this button (Required):

When you have entered the information above, press "Get Button" and the code for your website will appear in the blue box below.

```
Note : Copy following code and paste in a your HTML file where you want Re Squeek button to appear.
<script language="javascript">
                var button_id=14;
                var src="http://www.sokule.com/resqueek/iframe.php?
button_id="+button_id;
                document.write('<iframe src="'+src+'" height="145" width="100%"
```

All you do now is copy this code and insert it somewhere on your blog or website, preferably in a prominent place where visitors can see it. Then it should look something like this...

It is not that difficult to add this to your site and it is a powerful viral message distribution tool when you use it the way it is designed to be used.

Have fun.

There is no other Social Media site that exists anywhere on the net where you can re-tweet and re-squeek at the same time, which is why Sokule is Not Your Grandmother's Social Media Site.

Now we are going to take a look at my favorite communication tool...

Chapter 17 – Direct Message (Squeek) All Trackers...

By David Merrington - ('Moonraker') @Moonraker
http://www.sokule.com/postit/Moonraker

Many things come together at Sokule: social networking, business networking, network marketing, advertising, and even email marketing.

And what do all of these have in common? They have people... and they have communication. Sure, on the WWW we're all made of bits and bytes. But we are also real people, and we are in constant communication. And it's the **communication** that makes things happen on the web.

When we track someone on Sokule and they track us in return, we are able to communicate by **Direct Squeek (DS)**. Much can be said in the space of 140 characters (including spaces), but of course this needs some discipline, experience, and planning to do it effectively. It's a wonderful training in brevity and conciseness.

However, we also have another version of the **Direct Squeek**. Sokule members who are at the level of Bronze Plus, Gold, Silver, or Founder are able to use the **Direct Squeek All Trackers** application.

This is as close to email marketing as it gets. Every three days you can send your message to every member who is tracking you. If you have 55 trackers, each of them gets your message. If you have 500 Trackers, 1000, or even 3000 and more, your message will reach every one of them.

You message will appear in their email inbox and their Sokule members' inbox in their members' area.

So it's clear that **DS All Trackers** is a very, very powerful communication tool. In theory, if every single Sokule member was tracking you, that person would get your message.

We each have our own growing list of real people who have chosen to 'subscribe' to us—to accept our messages, to listen to us, to read what we have to say... and also to reply to us. We must treat those people well.

How to do it: The procedure...

There's nothing difficult or complicated in this. Go to the **Members' Control Center** and scroll down to the third set of Sokule applications. **Direct Squeek All Trackers** is on the left of the block.

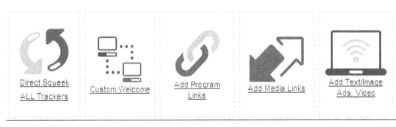

We are conveniently told when we can make our next DS. A timer on the page will indicate 00:00:00:00 if we can send out our message now. Otherwise, it will indicate how many days / hours / minutes / seconds remain until we can DS our followers again.

Click on the "Send Your Message Now" button and type in the message space as you would for an ordinary Squeek or a Direct Squeek. **DS All Trackers** provides 500 characters (including spaces), so it's the same as the ordinary Squeek for paid / upgraded members.

A Useful Tip...

Before you press **Send**, be sure to copy your carefully composed message. I have been caught out by taking so long to write my message that I lost it... when I pressed **Send** I was taken to the login page because my session timed out.

Another idea (which I always use now) is to compose all my important Squeeks, Tweets, text ads, emails, and DS messages in Word. The **Word Count** facility provides a count of characters and spaces used, which is perfect for our purpose.

Now the text is saved for possible future use. Simply paste it into the **DS All** space when ready.

Composing and Writing...

Think about the effect on your reader. There's a person at the other end... hopefully lots of them. You are not writing to yourself, or trying to convince yourself. Nor must it look as if you are trying too hard to convince your reader.

... And never, ever let yourself appear desperate for sales or referrals. Be courteous and civil. Be relaxed, kule, on top of things... and try to show that you have some interest in your reader. Remember that people feel flattered when you ask them a question, or ask for their advice or their opinion.

Then, if this is a promotional message, present your offer as best you can. Most affiliate programs provide varieties of text for our use. Sometimes this is great stuff; sometimes it's terrible—even illiterate. Fix it if necessary.

However, using the standard text can knock you right out of the ring. Every one of us receives the same lot of current promos from safe lists, hundreds of times a day. We know the pitch off by heart. We can see it coming every time... so don't be just another elephant crashing loudly through the bush. Be instead a nimble antelope, a graceful swallow, a wise and entertaining monkey, or a poised and commanding lion.

Visualize yourself and the effect you want to make. And try to write accordingly. Be remembered for the right reasons, not the wrong ones.

Try to be original in the limited space you have. Use subtle ways to make your **DS All** messages memorable and consistently you. One simple tactic is to present it as a regular 'publication,' as if it were a mini eZine. My method is to use a standard heading every time, placed above the text. You can also create for yourself a standardized salutation at the end.

You can even manipulate the shape of your text by using a hard return (i.e., the Enter button) to create shorter lines if you wish to look distinctively different.

```
Hi [fname], thank you again for tracking me.

I hope you are doing well and succeeding in your
online ventures.|
```
                                    [Click to send Direct message]

Avoid typos, especially if they will lead to misrepresentation or misunderstanding. (I remember once typing Hello – but somehow the 'o' went missing... I only found out when I saw a copy of my message.)

To sum up: Be human and social when you compose a **DS All** message. Try not to rush directly into a sales pitch. We have 500 characters at our disposal (including spaces). Use the [fname] tag. It works. And it makes a great difference. I read messages that address me by name. The others I delete without reading. You can always spare ten characters to type 'Hi [fname] ...'

Timing...

Every three days... this means we can contact our Sokule 'list' twice a week. Now let's think strategically about that. Let's think like professional email marketers...

Most people have time to themselves over the weekend. Therefore, it makes sense to use one of these opportunities late on a Friday, or any time on Saturday or Sunday.

We can try to visualize this even further: What countries, what cultures, what communities are likely to be at home and at their PCs on what day of the weekend, and at what time? And which country is likely to be the biggest and most responsive market for the product, service, or program we're promoting?

It is fun to speculate...

Now that leaves the midweek opportunity. It's commonly agreed that folks relax a bit on a Wednesday. The week's worries have been faced and it's downhill all the way. So, if possible, you should try to schedule Wednesday for the midweek **DS All Trackers**.

Marketing Communication: Best Practice...

How many emails do you receive every hour, every day, every twenty-four hours? Few of us count them. We have things to do...

But the more we get involved in the huge online community, the more email we receive. It can't be helped. After all, most of us are keen to send ours to as many people as possible... and the more the better. That's the marketing life.

On Sokule each of us has agreed to receive messages from Trackers. And this is a powerful pact. However, if we really want to make an impact on our community of friends, we need to consider *how* we communicate with them.

What **Direct Squeeks** do you routinely delete, often without reading them? Who is the sender? How do you feel about that person? What's the content of those messages?

On the other hand, whose messages do you like to see? How do you relate to that person? Do you ever reply to DS messages? And for what reason do you reply? For whom would you delay what you're doing and take time out to reply, to send a friendly message, a thank-you note, or a helpful hint?

This is the power of social networking, and it's the basis of network marketing. The Number One principle here is the relationships we have with others in our sphere of the web. And, if you've been online for even just a few months, you will probably agree that our corner of the vast WWW is in fact a very small world.

Every one of us is sitting on our porch, with the townsfolk passing, waving, staring, calling... noting and *remembering*...

This goes on even when we are sitting down to lunch, or fast asleep (do marketers sleep?), or climbing Everest. Thanks to Sokule and Twitter, for instance, we can be found in a Google search. People may see our beaming face; they can read something we said last month. Oh dear, they may read that nasty spat we had with someone six months ago... Yes, by creating a web presence we have made ourselves public property.

Lessons for Life in a Small World...

- Mind your step
- Mind your mouth
- Mind your manners
- Mind your reputation

Free Education: Learn from Experience...

This is where it gets interesting. And it's much the same with the thousands of regular emails that we receive. The "Delete" button shows the greatest wear of all on the keyboard.

But, among the next forty or seventy nameless messages, we see one from what's-her-name, and one from so-and-so, and another from Zeb (who has that helpful blog). Then we see one from Deb, from whom we bought that brilliant software last month. Yes! Among all the faceless stuff, Deb and Zeb are two friendly 'faces.' They do not get deleted. They have made it!

And then we see one from Max, the owner or the admin of a program we're in. That may be important. It may be essential or beneficial to us. Max has made it!

So, the best way to learn email marketing is to read your email. Make time for this occasionally, and actually—consciously—read them and take mental notes. (I even keep a daily Word file open for jotting down notes, effective subject lines, interesting turns of phrase... and also the worst stuff—what to avoid at all costs.)

We only learn by engagement. And between email and the internet we have plenty of scope for this.

Make full use of this self-education when you use a valuable tool like **DS All Trackers**. Don't waste the opportunity. Don't waste your reputation. Don't lose your friends by insistently forcing your favorite MLM on them. Who actually ever reads those solid wads of stuff about 2 x 4, 6 x 10 chrome-plated 12-cylinder super-charged matrixes and spillover, rollover, flyover, and what-not?

For me the worst is seeing the same promo made by the same person every time, week in and week out. What does it say to me? It says this individual has no regard for his or her effect on the recipient; i.e., no regard for you or me as real people... no imagination; no creativity; and no consciousness of the effect he or she is creating.

And, worst of all for a marketer, it suggests that this person has little to offer. Hey, if we've rejected that promo once, twice, sixty times, are we really going to change our minds suddenly and go for that worn-out thing?

You, Yourself, and Your Brand: DS All Trackers as a Brand Builder...

All of the above is ultimately about building up our own public presence, our web presence, our *brand*. Consider the first three famous-name marketers you can think of... chances are we'll both come up with the same names. They have... become household names; they have created their own personal brand.

Now consider Sokule and the people you know here. Which of them do you always think of instantly? Which of them draws your attention whenever you see them on the page, or when you receive a DS from them?

We must never lose an opportunity. In the world of networking, our primary focus is on building relationships. And this means that we work on selling ourselves before we get too involved in selling our products.

As we've seen above, eyes fall upon the trusted ones, the helpful ones, the friendly and civil ones—those who present an understanding and sympathetic ear.
Those who do not shout their sales pitch in our faces.
Sokule, among all its other attributes, is about Social Media. If you had a big dinner and one of your guests dominated the table, talking all night about the great real estate opportunity he has for everyone and anyone, would you ask him again? For me, he's a goner. He's destroyed any opportunity he might have had.

So do try to make space for a brief social paragraph at the top of your preciously valuable DS All Trackers, even if it's only one sentence. It could be a general comment on a global event, a festival, a holiday, or a news item. Alternatively, write something very brief about yourself that is pitched to amuse the reader. And let it lead to the offer you may be going to make. Go forth and communicate!

David Merrington, who really gets what Sokule is about, is one of our cherished founder members and is why Sokule is Not Your Grandmother's Social Media Site.

Chapter 18 – It's the Little Things that Count...

Social Media is about connecting with people in a positive way so that they get to know you and like you and eventually want to do business with you.

As in life, it's the little things you do at a Social Media site that get you noticed and makes you stand out from the crowd.

Sokule provides the tools for you to do just that.

Tools like...
- Edit your posts
- Auto welcome your members
- Wish your members a happy birthday

Edit your posts...

If you are a ronze member or higher, you can edit the posts you make. I insisted on this because I am the world's worst speller.

I can make a post on Twitter, for example, and 75 percent of the time, some spelling or grammatical error occurs that makes me want to hide my head in the sand.

At Sokule, I just take a look after I make a post, and if there is an error, no worries—I just go the box in the members' area that says "edit post," find a list of my posts, pick out the offending one (which is usually most of them), change it, and hit "update." Now I look like a professional poster.

Impressions matter and this great tool will help you regain some dignity.

Custom Welcome...

People track you at Sokule just like they follow you at Twitter.

If you are a Bronze Plus member or higher at Sokule, your trackers automatically get a welcome letter as soon as they track you.

They get a nice warm fuzzy letter from Sokule that says...

The custom auto welcome letter can be found in the third set of boxes in the members' control area...

The powerful part of this tool is that you can customize this letter in any way you like to reflect your own personality and your own business brand.

People perk up when they get a personal letter from you. It is their first contact with you and it makes a difference.

No one likes silence when they take an action. People have taken the trouble to track you. They want to know you appreciate it and they want to know it now. This is a powerful tool, so make sure you use it and don't be afraid to change it until you get the response you are looking for.

The Birthday Cake...

At the top-right-hand side of your members' area you will see a birthday cake. If you click on it, you will see which one of your trackers has an upcoming birthday. On their actual birth date, you can send them a card of your choosing and you can even add a gift of Sokens with your card, which drives people crazy.

They love getting a card on their birthday and, if you add in a gift of Sokens for them, they WILL remember you.

It takes about five seconds to send this birthday card.

Sokule sets it up for you so you can...

• Click on the cake.
• See who has a birthday today.
• Click on send card.

- Choose the card you like.
- Leave the default message in place or customize it.
- Add Sokens as a gift or leave that line blank if you just want to send a card.
- Hit send and you are done.

You have just given someone a reason to smile on their special day and I don't know anyone who won't appreciate that.

Sometimes it is the little things that matter. The little things you do for your trackers or list members.

Sokule has built into the way it does business the little things that count.
That's why Sokule is Not Your Grandmother's Social Media Site.

In the next chapter we will take a look at how you can advertise on Sokule and put even more of the green spending stuff in your pocket...

Chapter 19 – Advertise on Sokule...

Sokule gives you multiple ways to advertise your business and get your offers in front of our fast-growing member base. One key to making sales online is to get your offers in front of as many people as you can, and Sokule gives you some great ways to do that.

Let's take a look at them now.

The first step is to click on the icon that says "Advertise on Sokule" in your members' control area.

Advertise

Advertise on Sokule

Manage Ads

Advertising Tools

Promo Tools

Founder Offers

When you do you will see a page that looks like this...

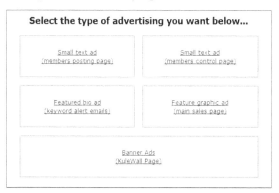

1. Small text ads...

There are two types of small text ads. They appear in different sections of the site.

One type appears on the members' control page at the top right of the page.

The second type of text ad appears on the members' posting page.

Both appear on high-traffic pages that should give you a lot of exposure.

Example: if you go to manage ads in your account—it's the icon right next to "Advertise on Sokule," and you can not only see your stats for the ads you have running, but you can edit or change them completely whenever you want.

Here are my stats...

Manage Text Ads

Buy New Text Ad | Manage Ad

Sr. No.	Heading	Type	Views	Clicks	Added Date	Expire Date	Action
1	Clickbank Pirate...	control	9236	235	2009-11-04	2029-12-04	
2	Sales Xplosion Rocks...	control	9735	283	2009-11-04	2029-12-04	
3	Make $90.00 Every Hour	control	32812	818	2009-11-02	2029-11-02	

The third ad has been running since the site started and is up to about eighty clicks a month now. It started slowly when Sokule first launched but now it is cruising. I just renewed ads one and two. They expired after the first month and I didn't renew them until now, as I wanted our new members to get all the action. Now the members' database is large enough to include my ads without affecting the returns our members get.

To edit an ad or completely change it you just need to click on the action icon in the same line. It doesn't get any easier than that. You can even see a preview of your ad so you can make sure it looks okay.

Fields marked with * are compulsory

*Heading:	Make $90.00 Every Hour	Max 24
*Body Line 1:	Guaranteed! Check out this	Max 26
*Body Line 2:	site now! It's Awesome...	Max 26
*Link URL:	http://janemark.com/likes/surveycash eg: http://www.sokule.com	

View your Text Ad display below

Make $90.00 Every Hour
Guaranteed! Check out this
site now! It's Awesome.

If your ad looks great above -
save your advertisement and we'll show it to all free members.

Save Ad

2. Featured Bio Ads...

Your featured bio offer will appear in rotation on one of our most highly visited pages—our login page. It also appears at the top of our Keyword Alert emails, which are sent each day to members who are tracking certain keywords or phrases at Sokule and Twitter.

This gives you DOUBLE exposure for your bio offer.

You can use your bio to direct people to your blog or website, tell them about an event that is coming up, or announce a product launch.

The kule thing about this featured spot is when you change the bio section in your members' area, your featured bio offer changes automatically in both the emails and on the login page. You are in complete control at all times.

Member Login

*Username

*Password

Login

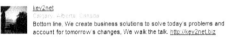

kev2net
Calgary, Alberta, Canada
Bottom line. We create business solutions to solve today's problems and account for tomorrow's changes. We walk the talk. http://kev2net.biz

Joined: 2009-12-15, Tracking: 443, Trackedby: 278, Updates: 875

Track me!

Login to feature your bio here

Use this space wisely. You will get a much better result if you have a profile that is friendly and informative, rather than a blatant sales pitch.

This is the perfect way to showcase who you are and what you do.

3. Featured Graphic Ad (main page)...

One of the most visible spots to advertise is on the main sales page. Right at the bottom of the page you will see some larger ads that rotate.

Sponsored by...

These ads are more expensive than the other advertising we offer because they are in a prime location and they get a lot of action, but if your advertising budget allows you to purchase one of the monthly spots, then this is one avenue you should consider.

4. Banner Ads...

The fourth way you can advertise on Sokule is by purchasing banners ads on the Kule Wall page. This page gets seen by all members the moment they log in—another high traffic page.

The prices are affordable and you should consider securing a spot now and locking in the current price as we are developing a plug-in for other networks so we can display Kule Wall on our partners' sites. The prices will go up when that happens, but you can LOCK-IN your price if you take action now.

You don't have to be Coke, or Pepsi, to advertise on Sokule. We have kept our prices affordable so businesses large and small can experience the power of Sokule, which is why Sokule is Not Your Grandmother's Social Media Site.

Chapter 20 - Promote Sokule and Profit...

Sokule is not just a Social Media site. It's not just a posting site. It's not just an advertising site. It's not just a site built for business. It is a business all to itself.

For example: Sokule has an affiliate program. You can earn sizeable commissions just by getting people to sign up and upgrade under your affiliate link.

If you don't have an online business, a website, or an affiliate program you want to promote, you can make Sokule your primary online business and start getting a paycheck from us every Friday.

Here is how you do this...

Simply tell people about Sokule and how they can advertise at Sokule too.

They can sign up free, of course, but many of your sign ups will more than likely upgrade at some point once they see the power of Sokule and how it can help them achieve their goals. When they upgrade you earn a pay check.
- Free members earn 20% on every upgrade
- Bronze members earn 30% on every upgrade
- Bronze Plus members earn 35% on every upgrade
- Silver members earn 40% on every upgrade
- Gold members earn 45% on every upgrade
- Founder members earn 50% on every upgrade

Now let's suppose that you choose to make Sokule your main business and that you plan to spend time developing it to the point where you have a monthly income coming in.

The next logical question is...

Where do I advertise Sokule so that I can get sign ups?

You are in luck. It just so happens that on April 6, 2010, we held a teleseminar on just this subject and you can listen to it and follow along with us as we reveal the steps you can take to advertise Sokule. http://philbasten.com/Sokule/ts/promo/

If you follow the steps in this follow-along link, you will get some good ideas on how to advertise Sokule effectively, as well as how to grow your trackers and upgrades at the site.

One of the most effective ways to promote Sokule is to simply tell people where you advertise and what tools you use at Sokule. Focus on one tool per email, and you may find getting upgrades is much easier.

Of course, your task will be much easier if you are actually using all the tools, and you can if you are a Bronze Plus, Silver, Gold, or Founder member.

Most Social Media sites do not offer you a payment when you bring people to their site, but Sokule is Not Your Grandmother's Social Media Site.

We believe you should get paid when you help us grow our site, and if you promote on a regular basis, we'd be more than happy to cut you a check every week.

Chapter 21 – Pick the Winners...

Most of us have certain people in our lives. Wonderful people who have captured our interest, provided helpful advice when we needed it, made us feel better when we were down, encouraged us when we needed lifting up, counseled us when we were perplexed, and mentored us when we needed to grow.

We like to follow these people and read their posts, their articles, and their blog posts so we can learn and be inspired even more.

A problem on many Social Media posting sites is that you have to search through pages of posts to find the ones you want to read. At least, it was a problem until now.

At Sokule we added a tool called "My Favorites." It's a place where you can add the names of people you follow and see all their latest posts on one page just by selecting their name. Let me show you how it works.

Look at the following image...

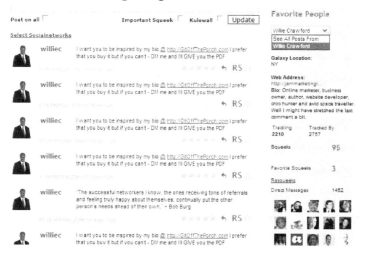

See the favorite people at the top. I added Willie Crawford, and when I select his name, his latest posts appear on one page where I can find them easily.

Now let me show you how to add a name to my favorites list.

Let's go to the search tool in the members' control area and search for the person you want to add. For the purpose of this exercise I am going to search for Ken McArthur.

I am not sure of his Sokule username but that doesn't matter. I can search on his last name.

Now I get this result...

See the word "Favorite" under "Message Ken McArthur" on the right of Ken's search results. All I need to do is click that to add Ken to my favorites list.

Here is my new favorites list...

Now both Willie Crawford and Ken McArthur appear in my favorites list.

I can add up to ten people in my favorites list and if I try to add more, then one of those people that are in the drop down menu now will be removed.

My favorites is a very kule tool that will save you a lot of time trying to find posts of people you favor.

This is just one of the many unique ways we developed Sokule so it would never become just your Grandmother's Social Media Site.

In our next chapter we will show you how to stand out in the crowd...

Chapter 22 – How to Stand Out from the Crowd...

By David Merrington - ('Moonraker') @Moonraker
http://www.sokule.com/postit/Moonraker

Add an image to your squeek...

It helps you to stand out from the crowd. An image will draw attention to your message. It can represent your personal brand. It can represent an offer you are promoting. It can illustrate some characteristic or feature of your product.

The possibilities are limited only by the digital images that you have the legal right to use. For example, you could use symbolic images such as a clock face, a star, the @ symbol, a green leaf, a stop sign, or a shiny 'Web2' button. Or you could use images of people—cartoons, stick figures, photos—to suggest emotion, action, and interaction. If permitted, you can sometimes use images from the website that you are promoting.

Prepare your image...

Don't rush into this—plan and prepare carefully. Digital images can be awkward things. An image may look perfect on your PC but terrible on a website. Or it may look tiny on your PC but much bigger on the web.

To make matters more complicated, it may look quite different on different websites. Sokule, like many other web platforms, prefers a square-shaped image. If it's not square, it may look distorted after you upload it.

Then again, different websites have different limits on the size of picture you can upload. (I am going to call this the picture's weight, and we'll leave the word size for another aspect of the image.)

What then are the requirements for uploading and adding an image to a squeek on Sokule?

1. **File format**: Your image must be in one of the following *file formats*: JPG, GIF, or PNG.

2. **Weight**: Its *weight* must not be more than 700 KB.

3. **Size**: Your image should be a small-to-medium *size*. (It will finally be resized to 75 x 75 pixels).

4. **Shape**: Its *shape* should be square, or as close to square as possible.

Note: If you want to learn more about digital images, file formats, pixels, resolution and all those technical things, a very informative website is... http://www.normankoren. com/pixels_images.html

... as you create your images you have to think of *format, weight, size,* and *shape*. But how do you change these without expensive image-editing software? Don't worry. Microsoft® Picture Editor, or Paint, or Picture Viewer will do the job. Another free program is Picasa®... provided by Google.

Let's say we want to use a photo of our puppy. The original photo is 900 KB, a fairly high-quality (high-resolution) image. This is too much *weight* to upload to a squeek. The limit we are allowed per image is 700 KB. That's fine, because we can easily reduce the *weight*.

Make a copy of the original and rename it clearly (e.g., SokPup_A). Take note of the original weight—in this case 900 KB. The size of this one is 12000 × 16000 pixels. We are going to reduce both *weight* and *size*. So, we open the image labeled SokPup_A in Picture Editor (or Paint, etc.).

Now we crop the image, removing all surrounding background that we don't need. We can crop it either square or oval. And save the crop. This will reduce the weight slightly... but still not enough. So now we are going to 'resize' the image. Click on 'Image' and select resize.

The simplest way is to do this by percentage. Try 50% and then save the image. Result: SokPup-A is now reduced to 600 × 800 pixels in size. And the weight is reduced to 142 KB. This will upload successfully to our squeek.

All set then?

Let's create a new squeek using SokPup-A.

First type the Squeek text.

Then click on the *icon* image above the Squeek box. The image looks like this:

Now a *mini-window* will open. See the example below. The Sokule icon is the default image. It is permanent and cannot be deleted and replaced. In addition, we can add five images of our own choice. Here you see one that is already stored for future use. And there is room for four more.

So now we upload the puppy. Here is the *upload facility*:

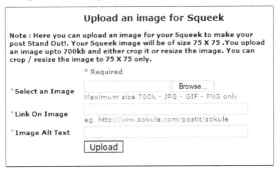

And here it is with the blanks filled in and the image selected in the *image browser*:

Do you see that the image even gets an active *link* in it? Any link of your choice...

Note that the 'Alt Text' that you type will appear when a user's cursor hovers over your image. Do you know what that means? You can use this to provide a subtle message, such as 'Best-seller for 2010' or 'To Your Success,' etc. In this case, I just used the words 'Image test.'

Next, we click on 'Upload'... and in a few seconds our image appears in the window. As you see, it is still much too big and must be either *cropped* or *resized*.

Now we need to scroll to the bottom of the window, below the large image and you will see the options **'Crop' / 'Resize'**:

If you want more control over the final look, select *resize*.

When the image is ready, the Squeek displays **'Image attached'**. All that remains are to click 'Save' and *post the Squeek* with the image added.

And here's the final result—a Squeek that has the user's **profile image** on the left, the **added image** appearing below the Sokule **username**, and the **text** of the Squeek appearing to the right:

Not so bad, was it? Try it now. You won't come to any harm.

Just note this: If you want to change one of your five stored images, you have to delete one of them to make room for the new one. On your older Squeeks, any deleted images will be replaced with the Sokule default image.

And here are some final tips on using images:

- Always remember to keep your original image and then alter **copies** of it.
- Use clear, simple, and **eye-catching** images with strong shapes and strong colors.
- **Contrasts** are always powerful—contrasting colors, shapes, light, and shade.
- If you want to use **banners** supplied by a program, they must be square-shaped.
- MS Paint and Picasa® both provide an easy way to **add text**—but keep it very brief.

- If you have Photoshop®, use it to erase distracting *background*; set this as transparent.
- *Store* your prepared Squeek images in a well-named folder for the uploader to find easily every time.
- Good sites for stock images are dreamstime.com, iStockphoto.com, fotosearch.com, and many more. A Google search for 'stock images' will fetch them. They will always have some freebies.
- *Never 'borrow'* a photo or a graphic from a website; it is theft. They often use tracking codes, and the consequences can be devastating... even if we were 'only going to borrow it for a day.'

Enjoy! Be Creative! And Stand Out From the Crowd!

Adding an image to your squeek sets Sokule apart from other Social Media sites and that's why it is Not Your Grandmother's Social Media Site.

Chapter 23 – Training, Unleashing the Power...

When you first open up Sokule, the wow factor will probably overtake you, excitement will build, and you may be tempted to yell out, this is SOOO KULE!

Well, go ahead, but just be aware that once the excitement settles down a kind of numbness will set in and you'll start wondering what to do next.

Don't panic. Help is at hand. At Sokule you are never left on your own.

First of all there is a large training section where we have created a set of short videos on all of our applications.

Training

In this section you will find teleseminar's that give you a broad overview of Sokule and some that go into some particular detail of Sokule. You'll find numerous videos, and as soon as my partner Phil and I can get to it we'll be adding Camtasia videos for those of you who learn visually.

Every day through admin you will get an email from Jane bringing you up to date on the latest Sokule News, and this same message will show in your members' area under 'Daily Message from The President.'

Daily Me ....
Invite your contacts now!

We have a tip of the day to help you use Sokule. It slides out on the left hand side of your main control area.

We have a frequently asked questions section which answers the most common questions about Sokule. You'll find it in the training section.

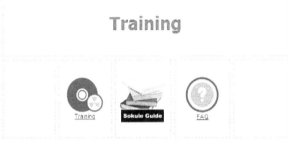

And if you still need help, we have a great support team that will get back to you usually within twenty-four to forty-eight hours. Just go to the link that says 'contact' at the bottom of the members' area and let us know if you need help.

And since Sokule is Not Your Grandmother's Social Media Site, this book can serve as a go-to guide that you can consult whenever you get stuck and you don't know the answer to a question about Sokule.

Chapter 24 – Founding Memberships – Simply the Best...

By Jenny Rogan - @jennyrogan
http://sokule.com/postit/jennyrogan

... why should you consider becoming a Founding member of Sokule?

EXCELLENT question!

Sokule's Founder members have an entrepreneurial mindset and understand that Social Media is clearly the direction that online advertising is headed. They know they are a part of something big... history making in the world of Social Media.

Sokule has been recognized by Business Investor Daily, and by Women's Entrepreneur. Jane Mark, President of Sokule, and Phil Basten, the developer of Sokule, have been featured speakers at various events, and Sokule was highlighted as a new start-up at the Open Mobility conference in San Francisco. In May, 2010, Sokule was represented again at JV Alert in Philadelphia.

The extensive reach that Sokule provides makes it one of the most powerful advertising sites on the internet. As a Founder, you have the finest suite of marketing tools, all in one place, and right at your fingertips.

Here is what you get as a Founding member.

- First, this is a lifetime membership. You pay one time and that's it.
- You pocket our highest commission pay out at 50 percent of each sale.
- You get a permanent listing in our Founding Members Business Listings, which could be worth hundreds of thousands of dollars to you.
- You get every application we create and add to Sokule free for life.
- You get to post on more than forty Social Media sites we currently have at Sokule, plus any we add in the future.
- You get the ability to ping the weblogs when you post your messages so the search engines can find your new content easily.
- You get a forty-eight-hour launch window on each new application that we develop so that you get first shot at selling it to your followers and list members.
- You get a special Founding members' seal. It is located at the top right hand side right on your Sokule postit page. This seal is linked to the Founder members' sales page, which helps you sell this membership.
- You get one million Sokens (Kule Coins) and you can use them to build your list of trackers fast at Sokule.
- You will be able to present your JV ideas to Jane Mark and Phil Basten. This doesn't mean that they will do a JV with you—your idea has to blend in with Sokule after all—but you will get to first base and sometimes that is everything.

Only 1,500 Founder memberships will ever be sold. At the writing of this book, the first 500 Founder memberships sold out. The price is now at $1799 for the next 500 memberships. You can secure one of these if you act now. Click on the upgrade button in your members' area. The price on the last 500 will go up to $2995.

You will be part of an elite group of members that stand out at Sokule. Sokule is Not Your Grandmother's Social Media Site. Founding members know its power. Join our very exclusive club now and profit.

Chapter 25 – Sokule, So What? – A Theme is Born...

Most Social Media sites don't have theme songs.

TV shows have theme songs. Advertisements have jingles. But Social Media sites, not so much. Well Phil and I said, "Why not!"

Why not commission a theme song to be written for Sokule. One that people could remember, hum, use as a ringtone to create some fun and interest in the site. But we also thought that if we were going to get a theme song written for Sokule, it was not going to be just any old theme song.

We wanted the best, so Phil and I approached Michael Mark from Michael Mark Music. Mike wrote the theme song for the popular TV show, Entertainment Tonight, which has been on the air for over twenty-nine years.

I bet if you stopped ten people on any street in the US, eight out of ten could probably hum the theme song for ET. We wanted the same thing for Sokule.

Fortunately for us, the idea appealed to Michael and he agreed to take some time out of his busy schedule and tackle the project head on.

He spoke to us on many occasions. His questions probed us more and more deeply until he managed to elicit the real essence of Sokule from us. Most of the time we answered with long explanations of what Sokule is and how it worked, but Mike kept saying, "No, what is the essence of Sokule?"

Finally, after all the back and forth, we realized that people usually end up saying one thing about Sokule and that was, "This is Sooooo Cool."

When people look at Sokule and get to know the site, they all say the same thing. "This is so cool."
So week after week we kept pestering Mike. "Mike we need the song."

.... and week after week I received the same answer back, "I'm working on it. You'll have it soon."

Well, as chance would have it, Phil and I were away on a cruise when the Sokule theme song arrived in our email account.

Eagerly, we downloaded it and started to play this long-awaited melody. The tune had barely finished playing before we knew we had a winner on our hands. Mike had nailed the essence of Sokule.

We played it for perfect strangers on board the cruise we were on. They clapped their hands and danced to this wonderful melody, even though they had no clue what Sokule was. They loved the music.

We played it for our members when we got back. They loved it.

Now it is up on YouTube. It is a ring tone on our phones. The air is filled with Sokule. Sokule rocks!

Listen to the song now and see what we mean.
http://bit.ly/Sokule_Theme_Song

To download it or make it a ringtone, log into your members' area and click on the icon that says 'Theme Song & Ringtone.' Sokule Rocks, which is why it is Not Your Grandmother's Social Media Site. You will end up at this page...

In the next chapter I am going to show you how to win friends and influence people.

Chapter 26 – How to Win Friends and Influence People...

Are you interested in people? Do you care about others?

If not, skip this chapter because it probably won't mean much to you.

On the other hand, if you are really interested in people, read on because you are a perfect candidate for Social Media sites, for Sokule, and for success.

Ask yourself this question.

Who would you rather meet up with on the street?

Someone with a smile, a sunny hello, and a funny one liner that makes you laugh? Or someone who hands you their business card and says, "I'm the greatest thing since sliced bread and I can help you become a millionaire overnight."

Personally I like the person with the warm, sunny disposition who makes me laugh. I am more likely to remember them than 'mister I'm always in sell mode.'
People with business cards and a ready sales pitch are a dime a dozen and almost always forgettable.

The reason Social Media sites are so popular is because people want meaningful connections with other people just like them. They want to feel like they belong, that they matter, that they are important.

For many years the internet was this overwhelming, anonymous, impersonal place where everyone emailed each other, but most of the time you never knew what the other person looked liked, where they lived, what they did, what they liked, and how their interests coincided with yours.

Social Media sites like MySpace, Facebook, and Twitter began to change that. People were hungry for a way to connect with other people who shared similar interests as them and the big three, as I call them, provided a way to that.

I assure you if you check the early posts at Facebook, MySpace, or Twitter, I doubt you would find a lot of posts like this...

Make Cash quick. Go to http://makecashquick.com

No one would have thought of making that kind of post when Social Media sites first started. Instead, people were eager to talk about themselves, what their lives were like, the interests they had, and even what they were doing at that particular moment.

Why?

Because they were looking to connect with others like themselves, and maybe form some kind of friendship, or business relationship, over time.

Time warp forward to the twentieth century and people still want to do exactly the same thing when they visit various Social Media sites today.

Hundreds of Social Media sites have sprung up over the past three years to meet this need. Some sites have specific audiences around themes like music or sports. Others sites focus on photo or video applications. Some allow you to post from your mobile phone. Some have maps so you can see where your friends live. Others are directed towards the business world.

But what they all have in common is one central theme.

Connectivity...

Making connections and developing relationships takes time. It takes effort. It takes a genuine interest in what someone else is doing and finding out what's important to them. It takes reciprocity. I give you something or do something for you, and maybe down the road, you will give me something or do something for me in return.

Sokule is a Social Media site that was specifically designed to help businesses and individuals to connect on the net. You can meet people in almost any business you are in at Sokule.

But just like Facebook, Twitter, or any other Social Media site, meeting people in your field of interest means connecting with them in a way that grabs their attention and attracts them.

Just like the person you might meet on the street, at a party, or at Church, you extend your hand to them and try to find out something about them. How you make your first impression with someone is critical.

You can leave that person with a memorable moment or you can make them go away shaking their head thinking—who the heck is that person?—Why would I want to meet them again?

Many business people online have a lot to learn about how to connect with others when they are on a Social Media site. You would think they would be smart enough to know that you need to develop relationships with people before you invite them to do business with you.

But, more often than not, you will see people who should know better just shoot ads out all over the net on Sokule, Facebook, Twitter, MySpace, and all the other Social Media sites hoping that someone will read their posts and buy something from them.

I honestly don't know why they bother.

No one is going to pay much attention to their posts when they are just ads, unless those ads meet a specific need or solve a specific problem. Try to develop something extraordinary, or unique, about the way you present yourself that makes people want to do business with you. You'll enjoy a lot more success.

So let's begin at the beginning...

Sokule is a Social Media site that provides a specific service. The end goal of which is to help you to connect with others in your own field of interest and see if the possibility exists for you to eventually conduct business with them.

Notice the words I am using.

They are all words that require your time, attention, and understanding.

"End goal"
"connect"
"eventually"

These are time words. They take time—your time.

Example: let's say I am in the Real Estate business and my goal is to connect with all of the people who are in the Real Estate business. These are people either in Sokule, or members of any of the more than forty sites Sokule posts to.

I could make a post like this...

My name is Jane Mark. I have been in the Real Estate business for over 20 years. I would like to share my experiences with you and find out what you are doing. Perhaps we can help each other. Interested? Direct squeek me and let's get together and talk. You can reach me here... http://sokule.com/postit/sokule

Or I could make a post like this.

I'm Jane Mark and I am a real estate asset developer. I need 25 limited partners, if you are interested contact me at http://sokule.com/postit/sokule

Now, if I were Joe Jones Real Estate and I received that kind of message it would not impress me one bit. I would not like a total stranger to be asking me to become their limited partner before I knew what their track record was, or even if this was a person I liked or trusted.

Here's the point.

If you want to win friends and influence people you need to take the time to make friends, and then maybe you can influence them. You put the cart before the horse if you try to influence people before you have won their admiration and trust.

Social Media is the perfect place to do business on the net. In fact, it is fast becoming THE place to do business on the net. But you need to let your old notions of peppering people with ads go.

You need to think creatively about your business and how you present yourself to others. You need to think about how to brand yourself in a way that would make others want to do business with you.

If you can get over the hurdle that Social Media sites are not like email, where you shoot out an ad and people read it and buy from you, you will stand a good chance to succeed in this fast-growing medium. If you keep on doing what everyone was doing in the twentieth century, you may find that your business shrivels up and dies.

So here are some critical things to keep in mind as you navigate the amazing and powerful world of Social Media advertising...

- You need to have a genuine interest in other people to have a successful business. If you aren't interested in others, you can't expect them to be interested in you. These people are your potential clients and we tend to buy from people we like and trust.

- Add your own picture to your Social Media profile, not a picture of your pug nose puppy, unless, of course, you look like a pug nose puppy or you are selling pet stuff. Most people want to connect with real people, not pooches, no matter how cute and cuddly they are.

- Post items that will make your trackers or followers laugh. The world is, for the most part, uncaring, noisy, and full of unpleasant news and personal disasters, and that's on a good news week. Give people a way to unwind and smile again. Heaven knows they need it.

- Post items that will help your trackers or followers grow their businesses. Become the go-to person when they need a question answered or a problem solved, and make sure the advice you give is free. Nothing endears you to others more than someone who freely gives of their knowledge and time and seeks nothing in return. It's an attitude that draws people to you like an industrial-strength magnet.

- When you finally do recommend a product or service to your trackers or followers, make sure you do your homework first and it's the very best product you can find. Yes, you may occasionally goof, but your friends will forgive you quickly if you have recommended lots of other products that were sensational and they worked.

- Use your words carefully. You can't afford to waste any. Words have the power of life and death.

Use the right words (positive words) and you can persuade others to take action. You can uplift, encourage, and make them feel important—show them that what happens to them matters. That they count.

Use the wrong words (negative words) and you can lose a sale so fast it will make your head spin. You can destroy someone's confidence and make them feel like a failure.
If you are a Sokule member you will receive our daily messages in your members' area. Emails that will remind that what you say and how you say it really matters to your business growth.

If you want to win friends and influence people, reboot your old ways of doing things, and start using Social Media sites to connect in a meaningful way that gets you to where you want to go.

Sokule always urges members to do this.

Day after day you will see my posts at Sokule. They are designed to help people get to know me and hopefully like what they see and hear.

Every day we work to teach you the techniques that will help you win friends and influence people, and get ahead in life, and that's why Sokule is Not Your Grandmother's Social Media Site.

Chapter 27 – Here's looking at you, Sokule...
Your Sokule GPS.

This chapter is really your map, your GPS to help you find your way around Sokule. When you get stuck and don't know where a particular application is located, you can always come back here for a visual look at Sokule

When you first log into Sokule, you will see a special wall we call Kule Wall (see chapter 12 for a full description). This is where our paid members make posts that can be helpful to new members arriving at the site for the first time...

When you continue to the members' area you will see the page below that asks you to invite your contacts from your email address accounts. You should stop and do this as it will help you get trackers or followers fast. If you have already done this, click "I have already invited all my friends" and this page will disappear.

Fill in the information below and we'll search your email account

M Gmail AOL Hotmail Yahoo

Important. We do not store your email address or password on our system. The information you submit below is 100% safe Select your email provider from the drop down menu

--- Choose Email Provider --- ∨

Enter your email account login information

Email Id   example :- user@domain.com

Password

Invite Contacts

**Skip this Step
I'll do it Later**   **I have invited
All My Friends**

Next you will be taken to the main members' control page. This is the heart and soul of Sokule and where all the moving parts reside. You will want to get to know this area as well as you can.

Here is what it looks like...

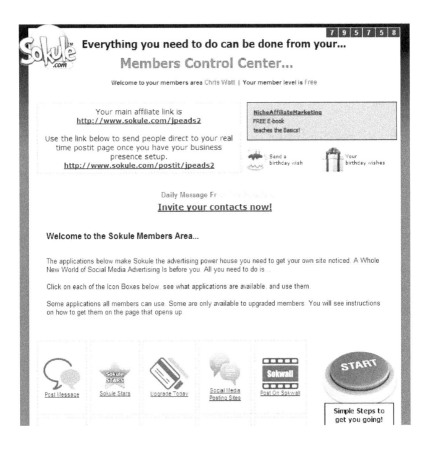

Each application on this control page is described, in detail, in one or another of the chapters of this book. This is a screen shot just to get you oriented.

Here are just a few of the main pages that you will want to get to know well.

At the top of the page there are two affiliate links. These are the links that will get you sign ups and help you earn commissions. You should know what they look like. Your sales page will look something like this...
http://sokule.com/[username]

... your postit page is the page where your bio, website links, and picture appear.

Your page will look like...
http://sokule.com/postit/[username]

... the 'post message' box is where everyone heads first. It is located in the first row of boxes on the left hand side.

Post Message

Sokule Stars

Upgrade Today

Social Media Posting Sites

Post On Sokwall

Our 'Sokule Stars' is next and then comes the 'upgrade' box that tells you what you get with each membership level at Sokule.

Marketing Tool Name & Description...	Free	Bronze	Bronze+	Silver	Gold	Founder
Membership Fee	Free	$9.95 month	$49.95 month	$297.00 annual	$697.00 3 years	$1799.00 one-time
		Grab a BRONZE position	Grab a BRONZE+ position	Grab a SILVER position	Grab a GOLD position	Grab a FOUNDER position
Generous commissions more info	20.00%	30.00%	35.00%	40.00%	45.00%	50.00%
Sokens (Sokule Tokens) On Signup more info	5000	10000	25000	125000	250000	1000000
Sokens (Sokule Tokens) You get When You Sign Others Up	25	100	150	250	500	2500
Auto-post on other sites like Twitter Facebook, Blogger etc - more info	Twitter	Twitter + 4	Twitter + 25	Twitter + 25	Twitter + 40	Twitter + unlimited
140 character posts more info	✓	✓	✓	✓	✓	✓
Auto-post on Twitter instantly	✓	✓	✓	✓	✓	✓
Auto-ping the weblogs more info	✓	✓	✓	✓	✓	✓
Find people with similar interests more info	✓	✓	✓	✓	✓	✓
Direct squeek (message) trackers more info	✓	✓	✓	✓	✓	✓
Add bio - tell your story more info	✓	✓	✓	✓	✓	✓
Edit your posts more info		✓	✓	✓	✓	✓
Add 5 live program links more info		✓	✓	✓	✓	✓
Add 5 social media links more info		✓	✓	✓	✓	✓
500 character posts more info		✓	✓	✓	✓	✓
Rotate profiles more info		✓	✓	✓	✓	✓
Custom auto-welcome more info			✓	✓	✓	✓
1-click direct squeek all trackers more info			✓	✓	✓	✓
Schedule up to 25 posts more info			✓	✓	✓	✓
Article length posts on Sokwall more info			✓	✓	✓	✓
Add ClickBank revenue stream			✓	✓	✓	✓

Many applications are available to all members. Some of the more powerful, server-intensive applications are reserved for upgraded members. You will see which ones these are when you click on them.

Get to know your way around the different applications. This guide will help you do that.

The various boxes contain the keys to your success at Sokule. They can open many doors for you on the net that have been closed to you in the past.
Here's looking at you; Sokule!

These applications make expert marketers sit up and say...

WOW! That's So000-Cool...

...which is why Sokule is Not Your Grandmother's Social Media Site.

Chapter 28 - The Real Story of Sokule...

Look around you.

What do you see?

Social Media sites are springing up like wildfires every day.

One thing is for sure, people want to connect with other people on the net.

They want to show off their family photos, their friends, their business acumen, their resumes, and they want to share their hopes and dreams with others. Sites like Facebook, Twitter, and MySpace were created to fill that need.

Sokule was born out of another need.

People wanted a site where they could reach other people with similar interests fast and effectively, in order to advertise a business online. Phil and I saw that need growing steadily over the past five years.

We run an advertising agency online. We have been doing this successfully for the past eleven years. A large part of what we do is to build lists. Large lists that our members can email their offers too.

We own and operate 268 lists with over 550,000 members on them. We host another 250 lists for other people.

Eleven years ago... when you mailed to lists, you could reach a sizeable percentage of those list members.

As time went by many ISPs, who got flooded with spam mail, overreacted and began blocking large, legitimate list owners and the percentage of people you could reach kept going down.

- Five years ago you could reach about 65 percent of your list
- Three years ago you were lucky to reach 45 percent of your list
- Today, you are lucky if you reach 25 percent of any list you mail to

Phil and I took a good look at this landscape and said: "We need a way around email. Some method that would enable us to reach members whenever we wanted to without getting blocked."

So we began to develop some fancy software that would look like email but would bypass email and reach all of our contacts without interference. We dumped a whole lot of money into research and development.

We even had a website setup called – "Side Step email!"

One day we took a chance look at Twitter and never looked back.

Twitter had the basis of what we were looking for.

- An instant way to reach people without getting blocked
- A way to connect with people fast and easily

- A way to put up a short bio and picture so people would know who you are

Twitter was great but it lacked one vital thing for us, and that was an easy a way for our members to effectively promote their products and services online.

Sokule was born to fill the void...

Our plan for the project was simple. All the business and marketing tools had to be in one central location. They had to work. They had to be easy and user friendly. They had to be affordable. They had to deliver members' posts to as wide an audience as possible. Based on what our members have told us, we managed to hit that goal out of the park.

Sokule is a powerful advertising site that gets your message out instantly all over the net. It's a great way to solve the email issue and it is just what the online business community needs.

Sokule is Not Your Grandmother's Social Media Site. We solve problems for our members and customers.

Chapter 29 – Our Members' Have Their Say...

We could go on and on and tell you how great we believe Sokule is, but that would be self-serving. We thought you'd much prefer to hear what our members are saying.

Jeananne Whitmer
http://www.sokule.com/postit/jawsie1951

Like many people, I had been stumbling around the net doing many different things. I had a blog, a Twitter account, A Facebook account, and Traffic exchange accounts. I even signed up for a course. The problem was I really wasn't going anywhere.

One day I noticed something odd. A site called Sokule began popping up all over the place. Traffic exchanges, safe-lists, blogs. It was everywhere I looked. It was playful and the owners made the task of surfing fun with a sense of community.

I signed up and logged in occasionally to see what it was about. It seemed to me at the time it was nothing more than an organized way to read junk mail. There was a lot of advertising, but no sense of community. People simply loaded their ads and went off to their next task, and I did the same...

So I fumbled around for a few more months but I couldn't escape the nagging thought that I should really get to know Sokule better.

Now I was curious and would log in more frequently, and I started to see the same people over and over. Not a lot of them, but a handful of folks that seemed like they were laid back, fun loving, approachable, and open to building relationships.

I decided to send a behind-the-scenes direct message (DM) to a few people to see what would happen. I was really surprised when they wrote back. I was a total stranger and they seemed like they really knew what they were doing and were making money like crazy. Why would they take the time to get to know me?

Well, this is exactly what I wanted to do. Make some money and have fun doing it with like-minded people. I realized that this is what I was missing from my community organizing days. So I really started to pay attention to what these folks were doing. They were doing virtual organizing. They were using Sokule as a place to hang out and share moneymaking offers from a personal level. It seemed like there was a method to their madness after all!

Members would "Squeek" a message in the main area of Sokule. The message usually contained a promotion for something they were selling or something someone else was selling. They seemed to do this frequently, some not so frequently. Some were long posts, some were shorter. It took me a while to figure out that this was part of a membership fee you could pay.

Next I noticed that they would send each other playful messages. Not secrets, but things that certainly heightened natural curiosity. Now I really wanted to be a part of this. The internet has opened the world but at the same time has created isolation, invisibility, and "virtual loneliness." Sokule seemed to help eliminate these factors and create a sense of community that I enjoyed in my brick and mortar career as a community organizer.

Sokule was more than I expected. I discovered it was a place to hang out with like-minded people, a place where you could ask questions and not feel like you were "dim-witted." a place where people would show you how to do it, actual tutoring that was not hyped or "mind controlling," as well as a place where you could trust that the help was genuine. Not just someone "trying to get into your wallet."

The next thing I noticed about Sokule was that it was always changing. New features would appear like magic, and sometimes they would be free. The one I liked the most was the Sokens feature. It was like a virtual game token or credit that you could use to get you trackers.

You could buy them, click on the stars by each members post and gain Soken credits free, or you could track others and earn them that way. The ultimate prize was to get to the status as a "Sokule Seeker" as fast as you could. You had to amass 1,000 trackers and offering Sokens was a super way to fast track your way there. The idea was the more trackers, the more people looking at your promotion, the more money you could make. Not a bad benefit to say the least.

There were many other wonderful additions, too many to go into here. I am sold on Sokule and I know you will be too. It's no wonder many of the internet's top marketers and business people are using Sokule to promote their wares.

After three months of clicking and networking religiously at Sokule I am happy to say I am in the process of building my first internet business. Finally I have a focus for my hours of clicking, waiting and watching. I met my two partners in the backroom... the posts and DM's of Sokule.

Tom Haley Success story
http://www.sokule.com/postit/earnincome

Sokule is a business-oriented Social Media program and a network marketer's dream! Sokule has a unique business platform with monetized applications that enable anyone of any skill set to earn money by simply sharing the concept with other people.

I joined Sokule right away at the Founder level for the many features and benefits, which I thought were most impressive, and I knew that whatever the cost it was worth it for the lifetime benefits and income.

Being a network marketer, I really liked the fact that I could build a following fast and I am also able to email them every three days for life, no matter how big my list grows. This has allowed me to build relationships and friendships with many business people that I would otherwise never have come in contact with.

I also particularly like the second website I received called the "postit page." This additional website helps me to brand myself with my team and on the internet with my photo and bio along with my business information including videos and banners. This additional page has given me huge success when advertising my Team Build System to my Sokule trackers and personal down-line.

Sokule is a also unique because of the immediate wide distribution capability of my many Sokule posts to the forty other Social Media sites available in the members' area, which also gets "back door" higher Search Engine ranking for any of my business posts to these other Social media sites... with one click!

Sokule is, indeed, a great Social Media program and a network marketer's dream to use and succeed in any business!

Peter Watson - Founding Member
http://www.sokule.com/postit/surgreen

When I first joined Sokule I wasn't sure what it was. I thought, maybe, it was simply somewhere to post ideas, thoughts, and opinions, possibly as a continual thread. As my familiarity and understanding of Sokule grew, I began to experiment with the different tools, one in particular called Sokwall.

I found this especially appealing as I could write article-length messages and it seemed there was no apparent restriction on the number of Sokwalls I was allowed to create.

As I began to experiment with Sokwall I uncovered a distinct advantage. I found that I could copy explanatory pages from within a site I was promoting and use it on my Sokwall page and enhance the pre-sell. People tend to buy more readily when the information you provide answers their questions and concerns.

I also discovered that I could create my own sales page on Sokwall and link my post directly to the payment page of the product I was promoting. A huge advantage as it meant I didn't need my own website.

The other part I really liked is that I could edit my Sokwall posts and correct any mistakes I made. This was especially valuable to me.

And finally, my favorite part, with every post I make I can ping an additional thirty-three weblog sites and let the search engines know exactly where to find my fresh content or post. Talk about getting free traffic effortlessly. Why not join me now and experience Sokule for yourself...

Jimmie Rose Bryant
http://sokule.com/postit/Inspiration

Sokule your life! That's what thousands are already doing. How do you do that? Let me introduce you to the one that can. His name is Sokule. You might say, so what? Let me tell you...

Sokule is a gentle media giant. Even though he is quite young, he has established an unshakeable presence on the net.

You see, all Sokule asks you to do is to Post. When you post, he Pings, and you Profit! How kule is that? Sokule, that's how! Sokule never sleeps. He works for you endlessly, 24-7, and if there were more hours in a day or more days in a week, he would gladly take care of those too!

This gentle giant is the most faithful companion anyone could ever have. Sokule is a perfect help mate/soul mate. He never complains, criticizes or tires; has no boundaries and provides an equal opportunity for all.

However, he would be the first to tell you the harder you work, the harder he works for you and the more profit you will make. Talk about the WOW factor!

Sokule reminds me of the words of a hit song, "Since I met you baby, my whole life has changed and everybody tells me that I am not the same."

Your life will not be the same either if you "Sokule Your Life."

Richard Brewster – Silver Member
http://sokule.com/postit/key2net

Increasing web traffic to your business is not easy. The internet is a busy and competitive place and getting the extra leverage to get ahead is not easy. An up-and-coming program that is offering great results is Sokule. This program allows users to post to many social networks with one click and, if you use properly, it can open up a completely new avenue of traffic to your site.

Search engines are also starting to index posts at these networks as links, which will increase the chances of your webpage to score higher in page rank.

This is important for webmasters because social networks are the future of traffic management.

Most people have an account in one or more of these networks and are more likely to follow a link sent by a friend than in practically any other website model. If you are serious about improving your traffic you should have a closer look at Sokule. There is nothing complicated about Social Media, it is simply a way of leveraging programs like MySpace, Facebook, and Twitter to get you where you want to go.

Millions of people use these networks and, if used wisely, can become willing sellers of your product. The beauty of this system is that people do not even feel like they are being sold something, they just think a friend is recommending a good product to them. Of course this needs to be done subtly or your post will come across to strong and scare off readers.

Sokule allows you to post your business message at more than forty Social Media sites with one click. It is a Social Media version of an article directory submitter and that means you can avoid all the waste of time and hassle associated with logging on to each network and writing a post.

As a bonus it creates a place for your company to advertise itself on this high-ranking site. Anyone bumping into your site through this internet site will instantly recognize where to get hold of you and what your business embodies.

The best thing about it is that it is free. You can create your own account and start using it without spending a dime. The developers work on the idea that you will enjoy the program so much you will want to upgrade to their paid version. This would not be surprising because this is a very powerful tool for serious internet marketers, and has the ability of saving you a lot of time.

The good thing about this program is that it can be as complex or as simple as you want or can afford. Each module that you purchase is charged independently so you only get what you need. For instance you can purchase the auto-welcoming module if you think it would be useful for your Twitter or Facebook account, or leave it out if you prefer to have a more hands-on approach to your networks.

Another nice detail is that you can make extra cash by selling this useful tool to other webmasters through their affiliate links. This provides extra incentive for users to use Sokule well and explain to others its strong points.

Jenny Rogan – Sokule Founding Member
http://sokule.com/postit/jennyrogan

When I first joined Sokule I thought, "here we go again... another social networking site where I have to spend hours yapping about nothing in particular, to everyone in general."

I already had a blog and had joined two other Social Media sites. But even logging into those three different sites every day was driving me nuts! Wow was I wrong!

Sokule has to be THE labor-saving device of the twenty-first century. Forget the dishwasher! One post on Sokule and your message goes out to more than forty Social Media sites instantly. The reach that Sokule offers from one single control panel is POWERFUL.

I can write Sokwalls that have at least the same power as articles, I can post information that may assist someone, somewhere, and of course, I can promote my business. I'm very grateful that I jumped in and became a part of this fantastic community. Sokule is amazing.

Chapter 30 – Summary...

You may have noticed that the title of each page is, 'Sokule – It's NOT Your Grandmother's Social Media Site.' We also end some chapters in this book the same way, and you may have been asking yourself why.

One of our members told me that she made dinner rolls in the shape of an "S". I am not joking.

Here is what Gabriella Darko sent to me.

"I see and look everything in 'S's now. I just made dinner rolls in 'S' form. Not kidding! LOL."

Sokule is... a place to meet people...
- A place to meet people.
- A place to have fun.
- A place to be creative.
- A place where businesses can establish a presence on the internet quickly and easily using extremely powerful advertising tools. Each application that we add to Sokule serves this purpose.
- A place to connect with others who are working in your field whether you are in marketing, real estate, or the health field. If you love music and books and the arts in general, you will find like-minded people at Sokule, like Gabriella, who love the site and are constantly coming up with creative ideas on how to use it.

Sokule lets you post instantly to more than forty sites. This is one of our most powerful advertising tools but to make it really work for you at peak performance, you should be using Sokwall in conjunction with it and post longer posts with rich content and keywords.

Sokule is a list building site, and to get the most out of your list building, you want to use the auto welcome letter to make your trackers (followers) feel welcome the instant they start following you.

The Sokule applications we have highlighted in this book are designed to work with one another to strengthen your advertising visibility on the net. Each application boosts your ability to make lasting business connections on the net, and making solid business connections is the way you make sales.

Social Media is fast becoming the optimal way for businesses large and small to reach their target audience. If you are not using it, you are burying your head in the sand and severely limiting your success.

Businesses around the world are flocking to sites like Twitter, Facebook, MySpace, and dozens of other Social Media sites to reach new audiences. Many are now flocking to Sokule where they can login - Make a post – Click submit once - and they never have to log into Twitter, Facebook, or MySpace or any other large Social Media site again.

Sokule—It's NOT Your Grandmother's Social Media Site. It has been designed for twenty-first century business on the net.

Come join us and prosper.
Jane Mark
Phil Basten
Sokule, Inc.

Chapter 31 – Afterthoughts...

Here are the things we thought we should mention but didn't want to include them in the main portion of the book.

Sokule is not a static site.

We are constantly adding new applications and new posting sites, as well as new tools to help you achieve the broadest possible advertising reach across the net.

Sometimes we develop sister sites to Sokule when we see the need to add in something that is missing or a module that captures some aspect of the online advertising and marketing industry.

For example, we wanted people to be able to get followers fast at both Sokule and Twitter at the same time. So Kule Track was born - http://kuletrack.com

...we also wanted to give people the chance to email large lists. Lists we have built over ten years and Kule Mail was born to fill that need – http://kulemail.com

...here are some more sites that are in development now.

Kule blogger
Kule Space
Kule submit
Kule Cash
Kule Zone
Kule Mania

Sokule is always developing new innovative products to stay ahead of the curve and help you stay one step ahead of your competition.

Sokule related sites and partners...

Traffic Geyser:

This is one of the best known sites on the net. You can submit your videos to many different sites through Traffic Geyser including to Sokule. Frank Sousa, our friend and former partner in Traffic Geyser, is our top recruiter at Sokule. You will see him at the top of the Sokule stars. One day I am going to beat him but until then he is the promotion king at Sokule. http://bit.ly/trafficg_vid

Swom:

New Social Media site where you can join a group called Make The Most of Your Sokule. One of our founding members, Nina Spelman, who knows Sokule like the back of her hand, has a group at Swom and she will help you with any questions you have about Sokule. I often stop in here to put my two cents in as well. http://bit.ly/swom_this_now

APSense:

This is one of the posting sites at Sokule. It is an interesting site with a Chinese owner that will give you access to whole new market. http://bit.ly/my_apsense

...you can join Swom and APSense free.

Membership Tips:

Many members ask us what membership we recommend when they are just starting out and have a limited budget.

We usually suggest the bronze membership with some key add-ons.

Here is our recommendation...

*   Bronze membership $9.95 month
*   Auto Welcome $2.00 month
*   Direct Squeek $5.00 month

    ... the total membership fee for this would be $16.95 a month.

We strongly recommend adding the Social Media add-on to this list which would take the total up to $31.95 a month.

Your ultimate goal should be to upgrade to a Silver or Founder membership. You get all the marketing and advertising power of Sokule and you'll save a ton of money over time.

Jane Mark   Phil Basten
President   Developer

Disclaimer: Every effort has been made to make this Guide as complete and accurate as possible. However, there may be mistakes both typographical and in content. Therefore, the texts should be used only as general guides and not as the ultimate sources of the subject matters covered. The authors, owners, members, partners, and affiliates of Sokule shall have neither liability nor responsibility to any person or entity with respect to any loss or damage caused or alleged to be caused directly or indirectly by the information covered in this guide. Additionally your earnings potential depends solely on your own skill set and abilities. Don't blame us—our lawyer made us add this gobble-de-gook. :-)